STOCK 63/4
G'OON 120
121
129
27-9
84
83

Trams in Colour
since 1945

TRAMS IN COLOUR

SINCE 1945

by
J. JOYCE

Illustrations from the collections of
W. J. Wyse, J. H. Price, Martin Rickitt
and others

LONDON
BLANDFORD PRESS

Made in Great Britain
Colour illustrations printed in photogravure
by D. H. Greaves Limited, Scarborough, Yorkshire
and text printed and books bound by
C. Tinling & Co. Limited, London and Prescot

CONTENTS

LIST OF ACKNOWLEDGEMENTS

The following list is believed to be complete and accurate, but should there be any omission or error, we extend our apologies.

M. Bacon
British Transport Films
R. Brook
K. Chadbourne
J. A. Clarke
W. G. S. Hyde
B. A. Jenkins
B. Johnson
Kingston-upon-Hull Museums
Leeds Transport Historical Society
Light Railway Transport League
H. Luff
R. B. Manley
T. Marsh
M. Marshall
P. J. Marshall
J. B. Parkin
J. A. Pitts
J. H. Price
M. C. Rickitt
W. E. Robertson
H. L. Runnett
J. Soper
C. G. Stevens
I. G. McM. Stewart
Tramway Museum Society
P. B. Whitehouse
W. J. Wyse
Worthing & Southern Counties Historic Vehicle Group
I. A. Yearsley

PREFACE

THE aim of this book is to present an illustrated survey of British tramcars during the period since 1945. Although in these post-war years the tram in Britain has declined almost to vanishing point as part of the urban transport picture, the vehicles to be seen in this time represent a remarkably comprehensive cross-section of their long history, from the earliest types to the most modern. It is an indication of their great variety that even the 160 or so examples described in these pages by no means provide an exhaustive coverage. The vehicles that are included have been selected as being typical, unusual or significant.

Hardly less notable is the fact that the majority of the vehicles depicted are still in existence. This is due not only to the survival of such undertakings as the Blackpool tramways, the Douglas horse tramway and the Manx Electric Railway, but to the growth of the tramway museum movement which has resulted in about a hundred cars being saved from the scrap heap. Most of these are static exhibits, although others may at times be witnessed in action, but the important point is that they have all been preserved for posterity. This book is therefore not only a memorial to an historic mode of transport, but a guide to extant vehicles which continue as reminders of the tramway heyday.

Obviously the preparation of such a book would not have been possible without assistance from innumerable sources, especially the many publications that have appeared in recent years detailing the histories of individual undertakings; some of these are listed in the Bibliography, to which the reader is referred for fuller information. I owe a particular debt to Mr. J. H. Price who read the manuscript and very generously gave it the benefit of his expert knowledge; anyone interested in the subject must be grateful to him for his numerous writings in *Modern Tramway* and elsewhere, on which I have drawn for much of the information here. I am also indebted to the photographers for the use of their work; not least to Mr. W. J. Wyse for access to his unrivalled collection of colour photographs, to Mr. Price for his guidance on sources of elusive subjects, and to Mr. Martin Rickitt for his patient cooperation in collating and preparing the photographs for publication.

In a few instances the quality of the illustrations may fall somewhat short of the highest standards, since the originals date from the period before colour photography for the amateur had reached its present stage of development; however, I feel that in these instances their rarity value makes them worthy of inclusion as historic records, for they are often the only known colour photographs of their respective subjects. While regretting that the absence of suitable photographs has meant that some other eligible subjects have necessarily not been represented here, I hope that the reader will approve what is included and not be too reproving of what is omitted.

INTRODUCTION

IF two qualities had to be chosen to epitomise the British tramcar the obvious contenders would be immutability and longevity. Somehow the tram always gave the impression that it had never changed throughout the course of its long life, and that it looked the same in every town and city in which it ran. Yet a closer examination would have dispelled any such impression. Certainly there were many enduring common features in design and equipment, as well as a typical British 'look', but the underlying theme was overlain by an almost infinite variety of patterns and details, while innumerable developments over the course of time reflected a gradual process of evolution.

The tramcar in Britain has had a long and chequered career since the American, George Francis Train, introduced his pioneer line in Birkenhead in 1860. Though the new mode of transport took time to establish itself and was not without its opponents, by the 1880s and 1890s it was an acknowledged part of the urban scene and was playing an important role in the development of our towns.

The horse was the first form of motive power, and although the early cars definitely showed the influence of American practice, home manufacturers evolved their own styles of that distinctively British vehicle, the double decker. Initially the top-deck seating was back-to-back on a 'knifeboard', but later the 'garden seat' was favoured, with passengers sitting facing forward on either side of a central gangway. The double decker was normally a two-horse vehicle, but smaller one-horse single deckers were also to be found on less busy routes. With the easier running possible on a smooth steel rail, the tramcar was a heavier and more substantial vehicle than the omnibus, and its capacity was greater.

Mechanical traction made its appearance with the adaptation of the steam locomotive to this new environment, and – in a few places – with the endless cable, but it was electricity which inspired the great boom of the tram's golden age. Blackpool had Britain's first electric street tramway in 1885, utilising the conduit method of current collection, while Leeds introduced the familiar overhead wire and trolley pole in 1891. Around the turn of the century electricity was going strong, not only taking over from horse and steam, but stimulating the construction of numerous undertakings throughout the country.

Indeed soon no self-respecting town could feel itself complete without electric tramcars running along its streets.

It was during these years, helped by the stipulations of the Tramways Act of 1870, which included such provisions as the power of compulsory purchase, that the local authorities came to play an increasingly dominant role as owners and operators of tramways. This hegemony grew as time went on, for the companies were generally more forward in moving out of the field; so it comes about that the majority of the examples illustrated in this book are taken from municipal undertakings.

To cater for the expanding market of the boom years, several manufacturers – outstanding among whom were Milnes, Dick Kerr, Hurst Nelson and Brush – turned out tramcars by the hundred, so that a number of basically similar types were to be seen throughout the country.

The standard pattern was the open-top double decker. It had a substantial wooden-framed saloon, with platforms built out from each end, rounded dashes with central headlamp, and curved stairways. Furnishings included longitudinal seats on the lower deck and transverse on the upper, almost invariably of wood in the earlier years. Although the open top had a remarkably long run considering the vagaries of our climate, the covered top was introduced at an early date. The London E/1, for example, was built with fully-enclosed top deck as early as 1907.

The body was mounted on either a four-wheel truck in the smaller versions, or on twin bogies in the larger. Though some makers constructed the whole vehicle complete, it was common practice for body and truck to come from different builders, permitting any desired combination to suit individual specifications. Standard equipment included such items as controllers and trolley pole, while braking started with the basic hand brake and went on, if required, to rheostatic braking, slipper brakes worked manually or magnetically, and later air operation.

Yet, fundamentals apart, there was ample scope for an almost infinite range of variations, and it is noticeable, at least after the initial flood of orders, that many local 'looks' became clearly distinguishable. There was no mistaking a Manchester tram for a Birmingham one, or a Liverpool tram for one from Newcastle, and in the metropolis, the London County Council's rolling stock could hardly be confused with that of the London United.

The larger operators, of course, were in a stronger position to specify to the manufacturers precisely what they wanted, as well as generally having the facilities to carry out their own modifications or additions to existing standard equipment. Moreover, many of them were sufficiently well endowed to be able to build their own cars to their own designs, and some of the most individualistic vehicles resulted from such local enterprise. The products of such municipal workshops as Manchester's Hyde Road, Liverpool's Edge Lane, Leeds' Kirkstall Road or Glasgow's Coplawhill established their own traditions and crystallised the distinctive appearance of their respective cities' cars. In later years, too, local enterprise was a necessity after outside manufacturers, faced with a declining market, had turned to other activities.

Though the great age of expansion was over by about 1910, the total number of tramcars went on growing until it reached a peak of some 14,000 in the late 1920s. However, in the 1920s and 1930s, the tram's dominance of the urban transport scene was ending with the advance of the motor bus and the trolleybus, both of which were now developing rapidly into efficient vehicles capable of handling busy urban routes, without involving the use of all the tram's costly fixed installations. In some cases these competitors quickly superseded the older mode of transport. In others they stimulated improvements to the tram; the traditional wooden seats, for example, had to be replaced by upholstered seats now that passengers were becoming accustomed to this standard of comfort on the railless vehicles. More powerful motors and air brakes were needed to enliven the acceleration and deceleration in order to speed up the service to keep pace.

Under these circumstances it is possible around 1930 to perceive the shape of the tramcar undergoing a transformation. Custom died hard, but after prevailing for some three decades the traditional heavy wooden bodywork was at last giving way to a lighter 'streamlined' construction which was not only more attractive to the passenger but was also more economical in power consumption.

If one design may be taken as marking this turning point it is the London 'Feltham', which incorporated lightweight bodywork, roller bearings to the trucks, air brakes, separate motormen's compartments, saloons unobstructed by bulkheads, straight stairways, platform doors and front exits. Nearly all these features were the exact antithesis of accepted practice, and even if all of them had previously been employed at some time or other, never before had they been concentrated in one vehicle.

In the ensuing years further advanced designs made their appearance, including such well-known types as the Glasgow 'Coronations', the Liverpool 'Green Goddesses', and the range of Blackpool central-entrance single and double deckers. Not only different externally, these designs embodied technical developments in motors, suspension and equipment, covering such features as contactor control to make the motorman's task easier and the passenger's journey smoother.

However, this modernisation took place in only a limited number of undertakings; the 1930s were a sad decade for the tramcar for its numbers were almost halved during those ten years. Many towns and cities decided that it should give way to the bus and trolleybus, in view of growing traffic congestion, the need for re-equipment, and the necessity to develop new routes into expanding suburbs without incurring the expense of elaborate fixed tracks. Once taken, this decision implied that the minimum should be spent on the doomed tramways in their declining days, with the result that old and outdated equipment remained in operation until the final closure, giving the impression that progress on rails was impossible.

With the larger undertakings the abandonment plans were necessarily long term, since considerable capital assets were involved, and the advent of the Second World War in 1939 called a halt to some which had not yet been completed. Thus it came about that in these places the tramways were given a reprieve for several years.

In 1945 the British Isles still had about 6,000 tramcars, operated by some forty different undertakings. These included the municipalities of Aberdeen, Belfast, Birmingham, Blackburn, Blackpool, Bolton, Bradford, Bury, Cardiff, Darwen, Dundee, Edinburgh, Glasgow, Hull, Leeds, Leicester, Manchester, Oldham, Plymouth, Sheffield, Southampton, South Shields, Stockport, Sunderland, and the Stalybridge, Hyde, Mossley and Dukinfield Joint Board; the company undertakings included the Gateshead and District Tramways, the Llandudno and Colwyn Bay Electric Railway, the Manx Electric Railway and its adjoining Snaefell Mountain line, the Swansea and Mumbles Railway, the Great Orme cable tramway, the Giants Causeway, and the Bessbrook and Newry. In addition there were three lines owned by main-line railway companies: the Grimsby and Immingham Electric Railway owned by the London and North Eastern Railway, and the Hill of Howth tramway and the Fintona horse tram both owned by the Great Northern Railway of Ireland.

London's tramways were operated by the London Passenger Transport Board, and Dublin's by Coras Iompair Eireann. The Douglas Corporation horse tramway was closed during the war but was reopened in 1946.

Some of these concerns amounted to little more than the remnants of systems which, but for the war, would have already disappeared completely; a few hardly witnessed the coming of peace in 1945. Plymouth's half-dozen cars which had struggled through the war years along one route said goodbye in 1945, while that same year also saw finales in Hull and on the Stalybridge, Hyde, Mossley and Dukinfield.

Among the others there were more small ones; if the extreme was the Fintona's single horse-drawn car, little more than handfuls were left in such places as Salford and Bury. Among those still relatively intact were the Llandudno and Colwyn Bay which could muster about two dozen vehicles, and Dundee with some fifty-odd. At the other end of the scale came a few giants; Glasgow with some 1,100 cars was easily the largest, London still had about 800, and Liverpool 750. Other substantial operators were Sheffield with some 450 cars, Leeds with about 400, and Edinburgh with 350: these, and a few others, up to now were not contemplating wholesale abandonment.

As the pressure eased and buses became more readily available so the process of replacement got well under way again to complete the frustrated pre-war plans. The end came in South Shields, Oldham and Darwen in 1946, in Bolton and Salford in 1947, and in Manchester, Bury, Dublin, Blackburn, Leicester and Southampton in 1949. Cardiff, Newcastle and Bradford followed suit in 1950, by which time the total number of cars had been reduced to well under 5,000. The next five years were even more gloomy, with this figure cut to little more than 2,000; final closure took place in Gateshead and Stockport in 1951, while the vast changeovers in London and Birmingham were concluded in 1952 and 1953 respectively. In addition, Belfast ceased in 1953 and Sunderland in 1954.

Yet even during the post-1945 years, when the tramcar was in this last stage of its eclipse, several new designs were produced, for some undertakings were still retaining systems that were giving good service. This was the case, for example, in Glasgow, Aberdeen, Leeds, Sheffield and Blackpool. Fundamentally, most of these new designs were advanced versions of pre-war models – the Glasgow 'Cunarder', for instance, was essentially an up-dated 'Coronation' – but there were also cases of the adoption of more advanced equipment such as resilient wheels and automatic control systems. There were also intriguing developments like the Leeds experimental single deckers and the introduction of trailers in Blackpool.

The new tramcars introduced from 1945 onward may be summarised as follows. By far the largest number went to the largest operator, Glasgow; 100 of the 'Coronation Mark II' type (better known as the 'Cunarders') were built between 1948 and 1952, while a further six 'Coronations' very similar to the pre-war pattern were added in 1954 as replacements for older vehicles. Still in Scotland, Edinburgh built a total of 18 four wheelers between 1945 and 1950 to its established standard design, while Aberdeen in 1949 invested in 20 central-entrance bogie cars of the type introduced experimentally in 1940. Then in England Sheffield produced a new design in 1946, and this led to a further 35 between 1950 and 1952. Leeds constructed an experimental double decker in 1948, and then in 1953 and 1954 tried out its three central-entrance single deckers, of which one was technically a rebuild. Blackpool introduced its 25 new 'Coronation' single deckers between 1952 and 1954, well in its modernistic tradition, while 1960 saw the coming of the ten new trailers. In addition, of course, Blackpool undertook numerous reconstructions which virtually amounted to new vehicles, to say nothing of the creation of several 'illuminated' cars.

Nevertheless, all these newcomers amounted to only a relatively small total. It was obvious that for such a limited market new vehicles had to be virtually custom-built rather than mass-produced, with the result that prices were correspondingly high. This was a factor which militated against re-equipment – and also incidentally stimulated interest in the second-hand market where some good bargains were picked up by the surviving operators as useful vehicles became redundant elsewhere. This problem of new vehicles allied itself with generally rising costs during this period of inflation to render the tramway, with its large amount of expensive fixed equipment, an unattractive economic proposition, especially where extensions or large-scale renewals were called for. At the same time, the increase in road traffic with its resulting congestion, made the routebound tramcar more and more unpopular.

Nearly everywhere it was finally condemned and then virtually disappeared as the flag was eventually lowered by the stalwarts. The demise came in Dundee and Edinburgh in 1956, in Liverpool in 1957, in Aberdeen in 1958, in Leeds in 1959 and in Sheffield in 1960. By this time the total number of trams was dropping below the 500 mark. The year 1962 witnessed the end in Glasgow, the last big-city system.

In former strongholds like these, abandonment implied a reversal of previous policy under the impact of changed conditions which were considered to render retention impracticable. One outcome of this reversal was that most of the new tramcars that were introduced during the post-war period were withdrawn before they had had a chance of living out their useful lives. For example, the Aberdeen bogie cars of 1949 were no more than nine years old when they were consigned to the scrap heap, and the Leeds single deckers saw only about six years of service; indeed they were not put into operation until after a decision had been taken to abandon the system.

Such brief lives were in contrast to the astonishing longevity achieved by some of the old-timers. Indeed there seemed to be no answer to the question 'How long does a tram last?' One of the classic cases was that of the Glasgow 'Standards', many of which were still going strong after a good half-century of toil. Hardly less remarkable are the Manx Electric veterans which are still running, virtually unchanged, after some 70 years.

For here was another point about the tramcar: one of the reasons it could last so long was that it was capable of enduring almost in-definite rebuilding and reconstruction. Half a century's service did not necessarily mean that the vehicles were unchanged from their pristine state; certainly many practically were (and those of the Manx Electric Railway still are), but others were altered to a form that would have been unrecognisable to their original builders. Again the Glasgow 'Standards' were a case in point, for during their lengthy careers they underwent quite drastic transformation to keep them abreast of progress. Starting as open toppers, they were gradually built up into all-enclosed vehicles and were given such refinements as air brakes, high speed motors, and bow collectors. Elsewhere there were com-parable transmutations and many of the tramcars to be seen in the post-war period were by no means in their primal shape.

Taken all round, the scene during this time presents a moving panorama of tramway history. Nearly the whole story is visible, from the earliest days to the latest. There are the typical British double deckers, some all-enclosed like those of Manchester or Stockport, others with open balconies like those of Bradford, and yet others completely open on top like those of Southampton. Then there are the untypical examples, such as the long single deckers of the Grimsby and Immingham, or the 'toastracks' of the Llandudno and Colwyn Bay. There are trucks and equipments of all vintages, from the most primitive to the most advanced in the country.

After the casualty rate of past decades it comes as something of a surprise to discover just how much continues to exist. For one thing, there are the lines still operating, for not everything has been consigned to the scrap heap. And what variety may be found among these survivors. Blackpool, the only full-scale electric tramway system, is an example of the modern aspect; here are mainly single deckers, some dating from the 1930s but many of post-war origin, as well as such novelties as trailers and illuminated cars. At the other end of the time scale come the Douglas horse cars in the Isle of Man, while in Wales the Great Orme cable line at Llandudno recalls another mode of operation. The earliest days of electric traction are exemplified by Volk's Railway at Brighton, and by the Manx Electric Railway and its adjoining Snaefell line, all with delightful period rolling stock.

In the second place, there are all the preserved tramcars. Since the war, the tram has attracted a body of enthusiasm of the kind enjoyed by the railway. It would seem by some kind of natural law that the amount of interest has grown as the subject in question has been seen to be on the way out. Whereas obsolete equipment used to be ruth-lessly scrapped without trace, we are now much more conscious of its value as relics of our industrial heritage. Hence, instead of going to the bonfire, examples of redundant tramcars have been rescued and restored, both by official and other organisations and by individuals. The net result is that about a hundred tramcars are now preserved, many of them in specialised transport museums, such as those at Crich, Hull, Glasgow and Belfast, where they may be seen and examined by the public (and, in the case of Crich, actually ridden in). These specimens run almost the whole gamut, from an 1867 horse car to a 1954 electric, and display practically the whole process of evolution.

Thus the tramcar is by no means extinct in Britain. Although it no longer occupies a commanding height, it is certainly not a dead subject. In view of the part that the tramcar has played in the development of local transport in our highly urbanised land, it is fitting that it should continue to be accorded this recognition, and it is hoped that the illustrations and notes which follow will serve as a key to the present-day situation as well as a reminder of a past era.

I **Ryde Pier No. 3,** built in 1867, is the oldest tramcar
in Britain. It worked on the Ryde Pier tramway until
1935.

2 **Oporto No. 9** is an example of the earliest species of
British tramcar. It dates from 1873 when it was built
for service in Portugal. It is seen here returning to
England as a museum piece.

3 **Sheffield horse car No. 15.** Dating from 1874, No. 15
is an example of the smaller one-horse tram used
economically on the more lightly loaded routes.

4 **Aberdeen horse car No. 1.** A representative of the
earlier variety of two-horse double decker, No. 1 has
'knifeboard' seating on the upper deck. It originated in
the late 1880s.

5 **The Fintona tram.** An Irish institution, the horse tram at Fintona was still working in 1957. The car dates from 1883.

6 **Belfast horse car No. 118.** Representing the more modern type of horse-drawn tramcar of the 1890s, No. 118 has 'garden seats' on the upper deck.

7 **Glasgow horse car No. 543** dates from the 1890s and was part of the Corporation's first fleet. Many were later converted to electric traction.

8 **Douglas No. 28** is an example of one of the enclosed cars used in bad weather on the famous horse tramway at Douglas in the Isle of Man.

9 **Douglas No. 40,** one of the smaller 'toastracks', is the type of car usually more in evidence in the summer along Douglas promenade.

10 **Douglas double-deck horse car No. 14,** now a museum piece, represents the double-deck horse cars formerly used on the Douglas tramway.

11 **Chesterfield horse car No. 8.** This was another small one-horse car. Built as late as 1897, it was destined to have a short working life.

12 **Portstewart steam locomotive.** This locomotive of the Portstewart Tramway is typical of the small loco- motives used in the heyday of the steam tramway in the 1880s and 1890s.

13 **Beyer Peacock steam tram engine No. 2.** Built in
1885 for work in Australia, No. 2 was larger than the
typical locomotive used on British steam tramways.

14 **Great Orme cable cars.** The Great Orme cable line
in North Wales is the sole surviving representative of the
cable tramway in Britain. No. 5 is seen here negotiating
a corner on the lower part of the line.

15 **Volk's Railway,** still in action along the seafront at Brighton, is a pioneer electric line built in 1883. This car is in the former brown livery before the present yellow was adopted.

16 **Blackpool conduit car No. 1** represents the rolling stock on Britain's first electric street tramway, opened in 1885.

17 **Manx Electric Railway** cross-bench car No. 32 was
built in 1906 and is still active on the scenic coastal
route between Douglas and Ramsey.

18 **Manx Electric Railway No. 21,** one of the larger
saloons of 1899, is seen here hauling a cross-bench
trailer. This photograph well shows the unusual corner
doorway.

19   **Manx Electric Railway.** Distinguished by open platforms, trailer No. 57 was built in 1904.

20   **Snaefell Mountain Railway cars.** Generally similar to its counterparts on the adjoining Manx Electric Railway, Snaefell No. 2 is seen here in its short-lived green livery.

21 **Douglas Head Marine Drive No. 1.** Another car from the Isle of Man is Douglas Head No. 1, an unusual one-sided vehicle with both entrances on the same side.

22 **Glasgow 'Room-and-Kitchen'.** The central entrance and the two saloons account for the name given to Glasgow's 'Room-and-Kitchen' cars, used on the city's first electric tramway in 1898.

23 **Fleetwood 'Rack' No. 2** was built in 1898 for the opening of the Blackpool and Fleetwood Tramroad.

24 **Blackpool 'Dreadnought' No. 59** of 1902 shows the distinctive entrance and double stairways, characteristic of this unusual type of car.

25 **Sheffield single decker No. 46** was one of that city's first electric trams in 1899. It is shown here in operation at the Crich Tramway Museum.

26 **Dundee No. 2** was built in 1900 with open top deck, but was later rebuilt into this form to survive until the 1950s.

27 **The Glasgow Standards.** One of the most numerous and best known classes of British tramcars were the Glasgow Standards. This is No. 22 restored to the open-balcony condition of its heyday.

28 **The Glasgow Standards.** Another example of this class, No. 152 is seen in operation during its last years. It displays the route colour that was a feature of the Glasgow cars.

29 **The Glasgow Standards.** Sights like this were once
familiar in Glasgow, with the Standard cars showing
their different route colours.

30 **The Hill of Howth cars.** The last electric tramway in
Ireland, the Hill of Howth line had cars in two different
liveries. This is No. 7, one of the 1901 batch.

31 **Hill of Howth No. 9** of 1902 is in the line's original teak livery.

32 **The Dublin Directors' car** was once one of the most lavishly equipped of tramcars.

33 **Southampton No. 45,** built in 1903, perpetuates the old arrangement of the 'knifeboard' seating on the upper deck. It is here in operation at Crich.

34 **London 'snowbroom' No. 022,** shown here, was equipped with revolving brushes to clear snow from the tracks.

35 **Newcastle F class No. 102.** One of the largest of tramcars, No. 102 has seating for 84 passengers.

36 **Lowestoft No. 14.** An open-top double decker typical of many British systems, No. 14 served in Lowestoft practically unchanged from 1904 to 1931.

37 **Cardiff water car No. 131.** Another unusual type of vehicle, No. 131 represented the services of the works department.

38 **Belfast No. 249** represents the general pattern of open-top car once typical of many British tramway undertakings.

39 **Johannesburg No. 60,** British-built to a typically British design, was one of a hundred tramcars constructed in 1905 for service in that city.

40 **Leicester No. 76** has been restored to an earlier state after more than forty years service. It was built in 1904 as an open topper.

41 **Prague No. 180.** A contrast to British designs, Prague
No. 180 typifies Continental European practice. It was
built in 1905, and has been restored to its original
condition as a museum piece.

42 **Glasgow 'cable car' (Mains Department car No. 1).** This strange-looking vehicle was employed in the laying of feeder cables for the electric tramways.

43 **Llandudno and Colwyn Bay Electric Railway original single decker of 1907.** The company's original rolling stock was as unusual as its route, and No. 17 was one of the single deckers with which it started service in 1907.

44 **The Sheffield 'Preston' cars** took their name from their makers, the United Electric Car Company of Preston, where they originated in 1907.

45 **London Transport E/1** was thoroughly representative of the London County Council Tramways and was one of the numerically-largest classes of trams ever built. No. 1025 is the sole survivor.

46 **London Transport E/1 No. 1395** is pictured in service at a change pit where it changed over from trolley to conduit operation.

47 **London Transport E/1.** Though the main batch of E/1s were built between 1907 and 1922, more were added in 1930, though these latter were officially rebuilds. No. 572 is an example.

48 **London No. 290.** One of the vehicles taken over from municipal fleets when the London Passenger Transport Board was formed in 1933, No. 290 was built in 1910 for West Ham Corporation.

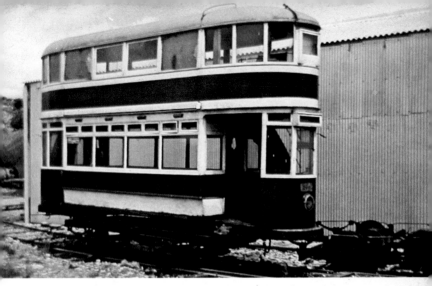

49 **Leeds ex-Hull No. 132.** Many transfers of second-hand trams were made from one undertaking to another, and one of the most interesting instances was that of the Hull cars to Leeds.

50 **Grimsby and Immingham Great Central No. 14,** in its British Railways livery, was one of the cars on the Grimsby and Immingham Electric Railway. It was distinctly unusual for a main-line railway company to run a tramway.

51 **Leeds 'Convert' No. 345** was one of a class of car that has been extensively modified during its lifetime. The cars originally had open balconies when they were built between 1913 and 1923.

52 **Fleetwood 'Box' No. 40** has affinities with certain cars of the Manx Electric Railway. It is one of four supplied in 1914–15 to the Blackpool and Fleetwood Tramroad.

53 **Llandudno and Colwyn Bay Electric Railway
No. 6** originated in 1914 when it was built for service
in Bournemouth.

54 **Dundee Nos. 34–51,** trams of characteristically British outline, were first built with open ends and later modernised.

55 **Sheffield 'rocker panel' cars** of 1918 to 1927, were the last of that city's cars to be built with the well-known rocker panels, for later cars were flush sided.

56 **Llandudno and Colwyn Bay Electric Railway ex-Accrington cars.** Five of this variety of single decker were bought from Accrington.

57 The **Sheffield ex-Bradford cars,** in their drastically transformed shape, still bear the Bradford stamp in the shape of their vestibules. This car was bought as a passenger car and then converted to works service.

58 **Glasgow No. 1068** was formerly Paisley No. 68 but had been rebuilt to look like a standard Glasgow car.

59 **Paisley No. 68** has now reappeared, as Glasgow No. 1068 has been restored to its original open-top condition and in Paisley livery.

60 **Llandudno and Colwyn Bay Electric Railway 'toastrack'.** Almost the bare minimum of tramcar, this 'toastrack' was popular in summer service on the company's scenic route in North Wales.

61 **Gateshead single decker No. 52.** The small single decker was comparatively rare in British practice: Gateshead and District Tramways No. 52 could trace its origin back to 1901 and is seen here undergoing restoration at the Crich Tramway Museum.

62 **Cheltenham No. 21.** Many British tramway systems made use of the open-top double decker, sometimes as the sole type throughout the history of the system. Cheltenham No. 21 was built in 1921.

63 **Stockport all-enclosed cars.** Most systems graduated to the all-enclosed covered topper, of which this Stockport car of the 1920s is an example.

64 **Stockport all-enclosed cars.** An earlier Stockport
four wheeler symbolises the traditional British tram in
the latter part of its heyday.

65 **Gateshead bogie single decker.** Another car in
British Railways livery, No. 20 worked on the Grimsby
and Immingham Electric Railway, but its native ground
was on Tyneside where it had belonged to the Gateshead
and District Tramways.

66 **Southampton domed-roof cars.** Though the deep
domed roof gave almost a streamlined aspect to most of
Southampton's trams, such as No. 8 shown here, this
feature was dictated by the need to negotiate a low
archway. The design originated in 1923.

67 **Blackpool Standards** were among the last of the
traditional variety of British double decker to remain in
service. This is No. 40 at Fleetwood.

68 Another **Blackpool Standard** is No. 49, this time with
enclosed ends and restored to an earlier livery.

69 **Manchester bogie cars.** An example of the standard
pattern of Manchester double-deck bogie car, No. 1052
is seen in service during the last days of the system.

70 **Bradford No. 104** was typical of that city's fleet, where the open balconies had to be retained on the narrow gauge. No. 104 was built in 1925.

71 **London Transport E/1 ex-West Ham.** Further members of London's E/1 class came from the municipal operators, including West Ham Corporation, whose cars of this class were constructed between 1925 and 1931.

72 **Aberdeen all-enclosed four wheelers,** built between 1925 and 1931, were the city's first trams of this type.

73 **The Leeds 'Pivotals'** were for many years a mainstay of the city's tramways; they took their name from their unusual trucks. No. 42 carries an earlier blue livery.

74 Another **Leeds 'Pivotal',** but this time in a later livery and with a new truck: many of the class were given more conventional trucks in their later years.

75 **Glasgow single decker No. 1089** was an odd one out. Built in 1926 as an experimental high-speed car, it was latterly generally seen only on rush-hour extras.

76 **Blackpool 'Progress'.** The decorated and illuminated tramcar played a part in enlivening the streets of many towns and cities in past year, and the tradition continues in Blackpool. This is 'Progress', built up on the underparts of a more mundane car.

77 **Blackpool 'Lifeboat'** was another illuminated car, again utilising parts of an earlier vehicle. In this form it appeared in 1926.

78 **Blackpool 'Gondola'** was another rebuild like the previous two illuminated cars. All three have since been scrapped.

79 **Blackpool illuminated Standards Nos. 158 and
159** also saw service during the period of the Autumn
Illuminations. They performed this duty from 1959 to
1966.

80 **London Transport E/1 ex-East Ham.** More of the London E/1 class came from East Ham Corporation, who had obtained them in 1927–28. This one carries the 'Last Tram Week' posters which were used during the final days of the London tramways in 1952.

81 **Sheffield No. 189** represents that city's tramcars as built between 1927 and 1936. Though the outline was familiar, less common were the flush sides and the curved glass of the end windows.

82 **Ryde Pier tramway** in the Isle of Wight had a history dating back to 1864, but in its latter years it was worked by petrol (later diesel) engined cars like this, which dated from 1927.

83 **Glasgow 'Kilmarnock Bogie'** of 1927–28 has the appearance of an enlarged version of the standard Glasgow four wheeler.

84 The **Glasgow 'Kilmarnock Bogie'** cars remained
basically unchanged, but No. 1100 was modified into
a form almost resembling the later streamlined 'Coronations'.

85 **Blackpool steeple-cab electric locomotive** was obtained by Blackpool Corporation in 1928 for the purpose of hauling coal wagons along the Blackpool and Fleetwood Tramroad.

86 **Birmingham trams** ran on the narrow gauge of 3 ft 6 in, and though there were many four wheelers, bogie cars were also widely employed and No. 668 is a typical example.

87 **Birmingham trams.** This view of No. 571 exhibits distinctive features of the design. It is running on the reserved track that was a useful part of the layout of several suburban routes.

88 **Blackpool Pantograph cars** of 1928 were so-called from the fact that this form of current collection was initially fitted. They were used on the Blackpool and Fleetwood Tramroad, and No. 171 is seen here at the Fleetwood terminus.

89   The **Swansea and Mumbles Railway cars** were the largest electric tramway-type cars in Britain. They were introduced when the line was electrified in 1929.

90 **Belfast Chamberlain cars,** introduced in 1930, gave good service on the city's tramway system until their last days.

91 **Dundee 'Lochee' cars Nos. 19–28,** the last new cars to be built for Dundee, date from 1930 and were the widest on the system, a fact which confined them to one route.

92 **Sunderland No. 52, ex-Portsmouth No. 1** was the last new tram in Portsmouth and was sold off second-hand to Sunderland where it gave many years of further service. It was built in 1930.

93 **Manchester's Pilchers** entered service between 1930 and 1932 and were Manchester's last new trams. They were later sold off for service in four other places; this one is in operation as Leeds No. 281.

94 Other **Manchester Pilchers** went to Sunderland, where they acquired that town's unusual livery as well as pantograph. Others of the class went to Edinburgh and Aberdeen.

95 **London Transport E/3** of 1930–31 was a development of the famous E/1 and was particularly associated with services via the Kingsway Subway.

96 **London Transport HR/2** looked like its contemporary the E/3, but it had equal-wheel trucks and four motors for use on hilly routes.

97 The **'Feltham'** of 1931 was one of the most famous of British tramcar types and incorporated many novel features.

98 **The Feltham.** With the decline of the London tramways, the Felthams went for further service to Leeds
where this one is seen as No. 519 in that city's fleet.

99 **Experimental Feltham, Sunderland No. 100** was
one of several experimental versions of the standard
Feltham. It was sold by London to Sunderland in 1937.

100   The **Leeds Horsfield** of 1930 was one of the neatest
of the conventional British double deckers. For many
years these cars were one of the mainstays of the city's
fleet.

101 **Sunderland No. 30** was one of a number of cars
purchased from Huddersfield. Built in 1931–32, some
were still working in Sunderland until 1954.

102 **Liverpool English Electric bogie car No. 764** represented an early stage in the development of Liverpool's more famous modern cars during the 1930s.

103 **Sunderland No. 86** appeared in 1932 and was followed by others of the type. It is seen here in the centre of the picture as the town's 'Last Car'.

104 **London No. 1** was the city's most modern tramcar. It was built by the London County Council Tramways in 1932 and was a break with traditional patterns. It is seen here working a 'special' in its last days of operation in London.

105 Leaving London, **No. 1** went north to Leeds, where it gave further service as Leeds No. 301 before it returned to London as a museum piece.

106 **Leeds tower wagon No. 1** is an example of the works cars which played an important part in keeping the tramways going. This one was specially built in 1932 for use on the sleeper tracks.

107 **Dublin cars** were large vehicles as a result of their wider gauge, but the last of them ceased to run in 1949. Here are two types – a balcony car and an older four wheeler – after withdrawal.

108 **Dublin's** most modern trams were of both bogie and four-wheel patterns, and one of the latter is seen here in a field after withdrawal.

109 The **Leeds 'Middleton Bogies'** were so called because they were designed for the reserved-track Middleton Light Railway.

110 The **Blackpool Railcoaches** were first introduced in 1933 as part of the system's large-scale rolling stock modernisation.

111 **Blackpool 'Balloons'** of 1934–35 were essentially double-deck versions of the Railcoaches.

112 The **Blackpool 'Boats'** were the third variant of the Blackpool modernised fleet and were specially designed for summer service on the seafront route.

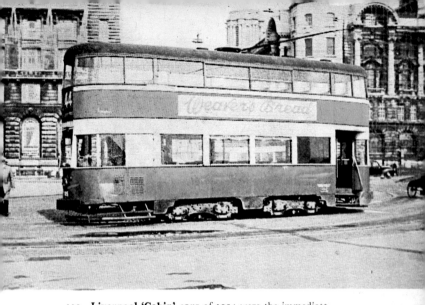

113 **Liverpool 'Cabin' cars** of 1934 were the immediate precursors of the more famous streamliners that were to come shortly after.

114 **Edinburgh Standard No. 35** was built in 1948, but these cars made their first appearance in 1934 and thereafter all new cars built for the city were of similar pattern.

115 The **Belfast 'McCreary'** car introduced in 1935 was
that city's most modern type of tramcar.

116 **Sunderland No. 27** was one of three cars dating from
1935. The curved roof lights are conspicuous.

117 **Sunderland's central-entrance cars** of 1935–40
were of an unusual design on a special type of four-
wheel truck.

118 **Sheffield domed-roof car No. 252,** the standard car
of 1936–39, is seen in a short-lived green livery.

119 The **Liverpool 'Green Goddess'** was one of the best-known of modern trams, having been constructed in large numbers in 1936–37 for the city's tramway programme.

120 An ex-**Liverpool 'Green Goddess'** in service in Glasgow.

121 **Glasgow 'Coronations'** were another product of large-scale modernisation and achieved a wide fame. One hundred and fifty were constructed between 1937 and 1941.

122   The **Liverpool 'Baby Grand'** was essentially a four-wheel version of the 'Green Goddess'. It was introduced in 1938 and No. 293 is seen as the special 'Last Car'.

123   The **Aberdeen streamlined four wheelers Nos. 140 and 141** were delivered in 1940, but bogie cars were chosen for later deliveries.

124 **Glasgow experimentals Nos. 1001 to 1004 and 1006.** No. 1001, shown here, was one of the cars built in 1940 to compare with the bogie 'Coronations'. No. 1006 was built in 1943.

125 **Leeds 'Austerity' car No. 104.** Leeds No. 275 was at first No. 104 and was built as a wartime austerity vehicle to replace an older car destroyed by fire. It is seen here as No. 275 passing Middleton Bogie No. 255.

126 **Blackpool's 'Marton Vambacs'** were an experiment
in adopting new techniques. They originated in 1939
as Railcoaches and between 1949 and 1952 Nos. 10–21
were given new equipment and a new name.

127 **Sheffield Jubilee car No. 501,** built in 1946, was the
city's first new post-war tramcar and was an interesting
development from the pre-war standard pattern.

128 **Leeds post-war double decker No. 276** appeared in 1948 and was the city's last new double-deck tramcar.

129 The **Glasgow 'Cunarder'** or Coronation Mark II, the standard design of post-war tram, was a development of the pre-war Coronation.

130 The **Aberdeen bogie streamliners** of 1940 formed
the pattern for the post-war fleet of twenty similar cars,
Nos. 19 to 38.

131 The **Southend Pier Railway** obtained new trains in
1949 to replace the old open-sided cars.

132 **Sheffield Roberts car No. 510.** The Roberts cars followed on from the Jubilee car No. 501, with thirty-five built between 1950 and 1952. No. 510 is shown here specially decorated for the 'Last Tram Week' ceremonies in Sheffield.

133 **Blackpool 'Coronations' Nos. 651–664,** built between 1952 and 1954, continued the single-deck tradition in Blackpool.

134 **Leeds Nos. 601 and 602** were two experimental single deckers produced in Leeds in 1953. These were the last completely new trams for that city.

135 **Leeds No. 600** was the last 'new' tram to be placed in service there, and was technically a rebuild of a Sunderland car. It appeared in its new guise in 1954.

136 **Blackpool's prototype trailer set** went into operation in 1958, utilising two converted cars as 'Progress Twin Car'.

137 The **'Blackpool Belle'** was launched for Blackpool's Illuminations in 1959. It was built on the frame of an older car.

138 **Blackpool's trailers Nos. 681–690** made their appearance in 1960, following the success of the trials with the converted set.

139 **Blackpool's 'Tramnik One'** is another striking example of that undertaking's illuminated tramcars. It was built in 1961.

140 The **'Santa Fé Train'** was even more ambitious and consisted of two vehicles. Again built on the basis of older cars, it went into operation in 1962.

141 **Blackpool's 'Hovertram'** was built in 1963 and was a further addition to the fleet of illuminated trams.

142 **Eastbourne Electric Tramways No. 2** was built in 1964 for the 2-ft gauge and captured the 'turn of the century' atmosphere.

143 **Blackpool rebuilt No. 611** originated as a Railcoach in 1935 and is an example of how a mature tramcar can be given a new lease of life. It emerged in its rejuvenated form in 1966.

144 **'H.M.S. Blackpool'** is one of the latest of Blackpool's famous illuminated tramcars.

145 **Eastbourne No. 12** is a modern-type car built for the narrow-gauge tramway formerly in operation at Eastbourne.

Ryde Pier No. 3

The tramcar has always been very much a vehicle for the masses, and there can be few trams that can claim to have been designed for royalty. But Ryde Pier No. 3 can make that claim, for according to tradition it was specially designed for use by Queen Victoria if she should happen to travel by way of Ryde Pier to get to Osborne on the Isle of Wight. In keeping with such dignified requirements, No. 3 was made especially decorative, its most notable embellishments being the corner-pillar carvings, the shapes of which earned it the title of 'The Grapes'. Also to be noted are the ornate tops to the windows, characteristic of many of the earliest tramcars. No. 3, indeed, bears the proud distinction of being the oldest tramcar in Britain. It was built as long ago as 1867, by a local builder in Ryde, apparently utilising some parts supplied by the famous Birkenhead makers, Starbuck. For a time in the 1870s and 1880s No. 3 was a double-decker, but it was then reconverted to single deck form, and it continued at work until 1935, being pulled and pushed over the years successively by horses, electric cars and petrol cars on the pier tramway. It was then finally rescued and pensioned off after this long and varied life, to find an honoured place in the Hull Transport Museum, where it may still be seen. Its native line, the Ryde Pier tramway, was still at work with diesel traction up to 1969.

Oporto No. 9

Like the Ryde Pier car, Oporto No. 9 is another example of the earliest species of the British tramcar, though of a rather less lavish design. It recalls the first of Britain's street tramways introduced by George Francis Train in the 1860s, modelling its vehicles on the pattern of the United States, where contemporary practice favoured heavyweight construction and ornate-pattern windows. No. 9, however, was not intended for British use; it is a survivor of a batch of ten built in 1873 by Starbuck of Birkenhead for the Oporto Tramways Company in Portugal. Here their first few years of life saw them worked by animal traction, but later on they were hauled by steam locomotives and even later by electric cars. Three of them were still on regular duties as late as 1959, creating something of a record for length of active service. By this time their historic nature had been recognised, and the Tramway Museum Society saw that one was an essential item to fill a gap in a collection of vehicles representing the evolution of the British tramcar, for no comparable vehicle could be gleaned in England. Hence in 1964, and with the assistance of Sandemans (whose interest in port wine gives them an interest in things Portuguese and whose advertisements now appear on the car), No. 9 was shipped to England and delivered to the Tramway Museum at Crich.

3 Sheffield horse car No. 15

Though the typical horse tram is generally visualised as a two-horse double-decker, there were many routes where the one-horse single-decker was quite adequate for the traffic and more economical to operate. Such an example is Sheffield No. 15. This was built in 1874, also by the then well-known firm of Starbuck, and it belonged in the fleet of the Sheffield Tramways Company. The system later passed into municipal hands, as did so many tramways around the turn of the century, and it was not long before electrification made No. 15 redundant in its original purpose. However, this was not the end, for its new owners thought it was too good to break up and they consequently converted it to electric operation as a works car. It served this mundane but no less useful purpose until, in 1946, it reverted to its former guise when the city celebrated the jubilee of its municipal transport. In 1959 it went to the Crich Tramway Museum, where it had the honour of inaugurating the first public operation, hauled of course by a horse. As with all progressive tramways, however, it was subsequently replaced by electric traction. No. 15 paid another brief visit to its old haunts in 1961, where it made horse-drawn trips in Sheffield along lengths of track that were still *in situ*. At the same period it was refurbished in its 1898 livery.

4 Aberdeen horse car No. 1

Aberdeen No. 1 represents the two-horse double-decker in its earlier form, with the then traditional back-to-back knifeboard seating on the upper deck. In fact, its origins seem to be shrouded in some mystery, and it can only be surmised that it first saw the light of day about the end of the 1880s. It still exists as a museum piece in the Edinburgh Transport Museum, and its survival can be attributed to one of those quirks of fate that single out one individual vehicle when all others that might have seemed more likely to endure have been consigned to the scrap heap. Thus it has come about that No. 1 is the sole remaining Aberdeen tramcar. It achieved its unique longevity by under-going conversion to electric operation in 1900 at the time when the city's horse-drawn trams were being replaced by the

new mode of traction, and for many year thereafter it served as a works ca Fortunately, the idea was conceived of restoring No. 1 to its primeval state as reminder of its halcyon days. It thu transpired that No. 1 was available to pu in an appearance on the last day of operation of the Aberdeen tramways i 1958, leading the sad closing processio along Union Street, and hauled – th newspaper reports tell us – by 'two sturd grey mares'.

5 The Fintona tram

For many years Ireland was noted for th unusual in transport, but few of its man varieties were more unusual than th Fintona tram. Not that the term 'tram should lead you to suppose that this was vehicle running through busy town street for to all intents and purposes this was railway branch line. Getting off the main line train at Fintona Junction, you foun that the 'train' on the ¾-mile branch t Fintona consisted of a double-deck tram drawn by a horse. This same form of motive power was used right up until th line closed in 1957, and so much of a loca and indeed national, institution had th tram become that when it was damaged i an accident in 1953 and threatened wit abandonment, such was the clamour tha it was hurriedly repaired and put bac into service again. The car was a genuin period piece; built in 1883 by the Metro politan Railway Carriage and Wago Company of Birmingham, it had knife board seating for third-class passengers o the roof, while the inside was divided int two saloons – each seating 12 – for first an second class passengers respectively. I later years, however, this rigid patte broke down and the vehicle became effe tively classless. (This class distinction wa more a product of its railway affiliatio for the ordinary street tramcar has nearl always been classless.) It bore the numbe 381, which might have created expecta tions of seeing a vast fleet of simila vehicles, but in fact it was merely numbered into the carriage stock of its owners, the Great Northern Railway of Ireland. After withdrawal, No. 381 went to the Belfast Transport Museum.

6 Belfast horse car No. 118

Dating from some time in the 1890s, No. 118 represents one of the more modern species of horse tram. Its three-window body – almost anticipating the typical electric car of the early 1900s – compares with the older type of multi-window design, whereas its transverse garden seats on the upper deck compare with the earlier knifeboard. Its saloon, indeed, is most handsomely furnished with red plush upholstered seats. No. 118 was constructed by the Belfast Street Tramways Company, and it was not displaced until electrification came in 1905. Thereafter it spent many years 'in the wilderness' until it was discovered doing duty as a summer house in Monaghan, from which point it was retrieved and delivered to the Belfast Transport Museum for restoration in 1962. It was mated with a genuine horse-car truck which had been used as a flat wagon in the Corporation's workshops, and a few parts were taken from another and less well preserved body which was also to hand, while new material was used to replace the items still missing. The result of the work is a complete vehicle which now reposes in the Belfast Transport Museum. It is in the livery of its original owners, and its authentic appearance has been enhanced by the addition of true-to-type contemporary advertisements.

7 Glasgow horse car No. 543

There can be no denying that, where trams were concerned, Glasgow did things in a big way. No. 543 is an instance of this, for it is the last survivor of a fleet of no fewer than 384 cars put into service by the Corporation between 1894 and 1898. Numbered 280 to 664, some were built by the Tramways Department themselves,

while the others were supplied by four different outside contractors. This great burst of activity resulted from the Corporation taking over the city's tramway services from the Glasgow Tramways and Omnibus Company in 1894, and then having to provide its own fleet of vehicles to run over the former company's routes as well as to serve new extensions. As it turned out, most of the new horse cars were to have short lives, for electrification started as early as 1898 and horse traction was soon a thing of the past. However, it seemed a shame to waste such comparatively recent vehicles, so when the need for electric cars was pressing with the rapid spread of the new means of power, 120 of the horse cars were converted into electric cars; they were given new frames and canopies, as well as new trucks, and were still to be seen in service until around 1920. No. 543 though was not converted, but was retained in its original condition by the Corporation until eventually it took part in the closing procession of the Glasgow tramways in 1962, after which it was put on exhibition in the Glasgow Transport Museum. It has an overall length of 22 ft. 6 ins., with seats for 18 passengers inside and 26 on the top deck.

8, 9 Douglas horse cars

The horse-drawn tramcars which every summer are to be seen running along the promenade at Douglas in the Isle of Man are a unique institution with a natural appeal to the visitor. To the transport student they are also a living reminder of a past age in urban transport, though some of the refinements, such as rubber-shod horses and roller-bearing-equipped cars, are well in advance of nineteenth-century practice and designed to make the animals' work as easy as possible. All the cars are now single-deckers, and each is hauled by one horse. The fleet totals about 30, and if this seems somewhat lavish for a line that is only about two miles in length, it should be noted that this number is sufficient to enable the type of car in service to be varied according to the prevailing weather. Thus for the brightest days there are the open toastracks; the large ones (Nos. 11, 12, 26 and 31) each seat 40 passengers, while the smaller ones (Nos. 10, 21, 38, 39, 40, 41 and 42) seat 32. For the 'not-so-bright' days there are their covered counterparts, the roofed 'toast-racks'; again these come in two sizes, the large (Nos. 43 to 47) and the small (Nos. 22, 32, 33, 35, 36 and 37). If the worst comes to the worst then out come the enclosed saloons, Nos. 1, 18, 27, 28 and 29; these are the more conventional type of tramcar with end platforms. Finally, to get the best of both worlds, there are three 'convertibles', Nos. 48 to 50; these have sides which can be folded back if not required. As is 'standard' on the island, the track gauge is 3 ft.

10 Douglas double-deck horse car No. 14

Though you can still ride on a horse-drawn tram at Douglas, you will not find any double-deckers there. This may seem surprising, since of course the double-decker is the traditional British vehicle and formed the major unit in the fleets of most operators. However, since it was naturally larger and heavier than the single-decker, the horse-drawn double-decker usually called for the exertions of two animals. In earlier days, Douglas was indeed no exception to the rule as regards rolling stock, but a more humane age found that even on roller bearings double-deckers were more than one horse should be required to move. Consequently, the year 1948 was the last in which you could have travelled on the top deck of a tram along Douglas promenade. No. 14 now stands in the British Transport Museum at Clapham as a reminder of that past age. It was constructed in 1883 by the Metropolitan Carriage and Wagon Company, and like many of its contemporaries it was given knifeboard seating on the upper

deck. It initially saw service in South Shields before crossing over to the Isle of Man. Here it was active until 1948, and it then returned to the mainland in 1956.

11 Chesterfield horse car No. 8

The rapid electrification of tramways around the turn of the century rendered the old horse cars redundant, and like the animals which drew them many were literally turned out to grass. Left standing in fields as hen houses or tool sheds, the cars eventually fell to pieces under the ravages of weather and time and so were never heard of again. However, the tramcar is usually a solid piece of work that can endure any amount of rough treatment, and odd examples have survived to tell the tale. Such a one is Chesterfield No. 8. This served as a summer house on a farm for over 40 years before it was rescued by the Corporation Transport Department and restored to its former state. In 1956 it was handed over to the British Transport Commission to take its place as an exhibit in the British Transport Museum at Clapham. No. 8 is a small single-horse car, and it is a fairly late example as horse trams go. It was built in 1897, the year that the Chesterfield tramways were taken over by the Corporation. Its builder was the famous firm of Milnes. Coming on the scene so late in the day, No. 8 had a very short working life, for in 1904 it was ousted by the new electric cars, and with its companions it was sold off for non-transport purposes.

12 Portstewart steam locomotive

Steam power on tramways enjoyed a fairly brief heyday during the 1880s and 1890s, before it was superseded by electric traction, and this Portstewart locomotive is typical of the kind of engines employed. Hauling a double-deck bogie trailer, it epitomised the height of urban transport at this period. Portstewart locomotives Nos. 1 and 2 were both built by the then well-known firm of Kitsons of Leeds, No. 1

n 1882 and No. 2 a year later. Both have the 0-4-0 wheel arrangement, and have cylinders of $7\frac{1}{2}$ ins. diameter by 12 ins. stroke; the wheelbase is 5 ft. and the wheels have a diameter of 2 ft. $4\frac{1}{2}$ ins. Track gauge is the narrow one of 3 ft. Total weight in working order is some tons. Coke was used as fuel, because Board of Trade regulations were very severe about the emission of smoke and steam, as well as noise. The regulations also accounted for the appearance of the machine, for it was decreed that the works' should be enclosed to within a few inches of the ground, not only to prevent anyone getting caught underneath, but to prevent nervous horses or pedestrians from being frightened by the movement of wheels, cranks and coupling rods. Most steam tramways were electrified by the early years of this century, but the Port-stewart Tramway was not strictly an urban line but connected the town of Portstewart with its railway station; although electrification was considered, the line went on serving its purpose with its original motive power until it finally closed as late as 1926. Locomotive No. 1 is now in the Hull Transport Museum and No. 2 in the Belfast Transport Museum.

3 **Beyer Peacock steam tram engine No. 2**
Beyer Peacock No. 2 is not really typical of the locomotives used on steam-worked street tramways in this country. Not only has it the distinction of still existing in working order, and still occasionally being worked, but it has travelled to the other side of the world and was doing a regular day's work right up to 1959. It was built to the Wilkinson patent design by Beyer Peacock at their Gorton works in 1885 specifically as an export job, for turning the scales at some 16 tons it was a good deal more substantial than models destined for the home market. It was sent out to Australia by the company for trials on the tramways of New South Wales where the loads it was expected to pull were much heavier than in Britain. However, its antipodean sojourn was brief, for it was back in England in 1890, after which it was 'railwayised' with buffers and three-link couplings for the purposes of serving as a shunting engine in Beyer Peacock's own works. It was performing this duty as late as 1959, and after withdrawal it went to the Crich Tramway Museum where it may still be seen. Its features include the Wilkinson-patent exhaust superheater and gear drive to the wheels. It has two cylinders of $9\frac{1}{2}$ ins. diameter by 12 ins. stroke, Stephenson link motion, and driving wheels of 30 ins. diameter.

14 **Great Orme cable cars**
In pre-electric days, cable traction enjoyed some favour on tramways, especially where steep gradients were encountered, but on most such lines electricity later took over. It is therefore something of a surprise to find that one cable tramway still operates – up the Great Orme at Llandudno in North Wales. Certainly it differs from the true cable tramway in that the cars are permanently attached to the cable, so that working is in the nature of a funicular, with one car coming down as the other goes up, but its survival is no less remarkable. Also remarkable is the fact that the original cars are still in operation; they are Nos. 4 and 5 on the lower part of the line, dating from 1902, and Nos. 6 and 7 on the upper part, dating from 1903. Built by Hurst Nelson, they are bogie single-deckers with seats for 48 passengers. Both platforms are open, and the windows are also unglazed, enabling the passengers to enjoy the view to the full. Obviously on a line where there are gradients as steep as 1 in 4, brakes are of prime importance, and apart from the more conventional wheel brakes, the cars are fitted with skid or slipper brakes to bear on the surface of the road or track in case of emergency. An unusual feature is that the cars are equipped with trolley poles, and an

overhead wire runs the length of the line; though this may give the impression that this is an electric tramway, in fact the wire is used for signalling and telephone purposes, in order that the drivers can communicate with the winding house from which the cables are controlled.

15 Volk's Railway

Though strictly speaking not a tramway in the usually accepted sense of the term, Volk's Railway on the Brighton seafront merits inclusion here as England's pioneer electric railway. It was opened by Magnus Volk as long ago as 1883, as a 2 ft. gauge line using 'two rail' current collection, a mode of operation now familiar to present-day railway modellers but obviously having a very respectable ancestry. It was later converted to 2 ft. 9 ins. gauge (it is now 2 ft. 8½ ins.) and the method of current collection was altered to a third rail laid between the running rails. The railway is now owned and operated by Brighton Corporation, and is 1¼ miles in length, stretching from the Aquarium to Black Rock. The fleet totals nine cars (now neatly numbered 1 to 9), most of which can trace their lineage back to around the turn of the century. However, they have been much rebuilt during the course of their long lives, though they have fortunately retained their considerable vintage charm. Nos. 1 and 2 are open-sided, cross-bench cars, whereas Nos. 3 to 7 have a small central saloon with sliding doors. Seats are provided for 40 passengers. Nos. 8 and 9 are also open sided, but were obtained second-hand from the Southend Pier railway. Modifications which have been carried out in recent years include the moving of the controller from a position above the driver's head to a more orthodox position, and the adaptation of the cars for working coupled together in pairs.

16 Blackpool conduit car No. 1

In 1885 Blackpool opened England's first electric street tramway. Not only is the original route along the promenade still served by the Corporation's modern trams cars, but one of the 1885 cars still exists in the shape of No. 1. This pioneer vehicle was built by the Lancaster Carriage and Wagon Company, and was at first powered by one motor which drove on to both axles by means of chains. In its early years the tramway made use of the conduit method of current collection, in which the conductor rails were laid beneath the track and a 'plough' on the car made contact with them through a slot between the running rails. This method of operation (which in an improved form was later much used in London) was given up by Blackpool in 1899, when the more familiar system of overhead wire was installed. When this took place, this car was not only provided with the necessary trolley pole, but was given a new truck which was powered by two motors. It continued to carry passengers until 1912 after which it was transferred to the less glamorous tasks of the works department where it undertook the roles of an overhead repair vehicle and, later, a snow-plough. It returned to the limelight in 1960, when together with three other veterans (the Fleetwood 'Rack' and 'Box' and the 'Dreadnought') it was restored to former glory – suitably emblazoned with the legend 'The first electric street tram-car in Britain' – to take part in the celebrations to mark the 75th anniversary of electric tramway operation in Blackpool. No. 1 is now in the British Transport Museum at Clapham, on loan from the Crich Tramway Museum.

17, 18, 19 Manx Electric Railway

Few electric lines have attained the fame of the Manx Electric Railway with its route between Douglas and Ramsey, and no little part of its attraction is attributable to the character of its rolling stock. The fleet comprises two dozen each of motors and trailers, and within each of these categories there are two main types: cross-bench and saloon. It is naturally the open-sided, cross-bench cars that are the more popular in fine summer weather when the M.E.R. attracts its greatest patronage for the scenic coastal ride, but the saloons are a valued stand-by when the weather is not so good, and of course they are the basis of winter running. What they all have in common is their venerable age, which makes them unique period pieces, while their superb condition makes them a joy to travel in.

Nos. 1 and 2 are two of the 'originals' dating from 1893; they were built by Milnes on Brush trucks and have open-ended platforms. All the other saloons have enclosed platforms with the unusual corner doorways; Nos. 5, 6, 7 and 9 date from 1894 and were also built by Milnes on Brush trucks, and Nos. 19 to 22 are larger saloons of 1899 with Milnes bodies on Brill trucks. The cross-bench cars include Nos. 14 to 18, built by Milnes in 1898; all have Milnes trucks, except No. 16 which is on Brush trucks. Nos. 25, 26 and 27 were originally trailers; they were built by Milnes in 1898 and have Brush trucks. Nos. 28 to 31 were built in 1904 by the United Electric Car Company (U.E.C.) on Milnes trucks. Nos. 32 and 33 are the newest motor cars, having been built in 1906 by U.E.C. on Brill trucks. Of the trailers, all but three are also of the cross-bench type. They are Nos. 49 to 54 which date from 1893; Nos. 36 and 37 from 1894; No. 60 from 1896; Nos. 42 and 43 from 1903; Nos. 55 and 56 from 1904; Nos. 61 and 62 from 1906; Nos. 40, 41 and 44 were constructed as late as 1930 to replace earlier vehicles which had been destroyed in a fire. The three saloon trailers are Nos. 57 and 58 dating from 1904, and No. 59 which originated in 1895 and is a smaller vehicle, which once had the honour of conveying royalty.

20 **Snaefell Mountain Railway cars**
The cars of the Snaefell Mountain Rail-way look much like those of the Manx Electric, with their unusual layout of corner entrances. However, there are certain differences, which arise mainly from the nature of the precipitous route which the Snaefell cars have to negotiate to approach the highest point in the Isle of Man. One obvious difference is that the Snaefell cars each have two bow collectors, instead of a trolley pole like their M.E.R. colleagues. This is to obviate the possibility of the collector being blown off the wire along the more windswept sections of the line. Another difference is clear from a glance at the track, even if not to be immediately perceived on the vehicles themselves. For between the running rails is a third rail, the 'Fell' rail, and the cars are fitted with wheels and shoes to grip this rail in order to keep them on the track and to provide additional braking on the steep gradients. The presence of the 'Fell' rail is believed to have determined that the gauge of the Snaefell line had to be fixed at 3 ft. 6 ins. instead of the 3 ft. of the 'main line'; it is possible to see 'mixed gauge' at Laxey, where the Snae-fell line at its lower terminus meets the M.E.R. There are six Snaefell cars, numbered 1 to 6 and dating from the opening of the mountain railway in 1895. They are Milnes-built, 48-seaters powered by four 25-h.p. motors.

21 **Douglas Head Marine Drive No. 1**
You might not have expected to find a fleet of old tramcars marooned high up on the edge of a cliff, but for a number of years you could have found just that if you had gone to the Isle of Man and ventured on to the Douglas Head Marine Drive. From 1896 to 1939 an electric tramway ran along the Marine Drive, offering a spectacular ride along the rocky coast, and when the line closed with the outbreak of war the cars were left standing in their isolated depot about half-way along the route. The tramway never reopened, and it was not until 1951 that venturesome

enthusiasts succeeded in moving one of the cars out of its eyrie and eventually getting it to the British Transport Museum at Clapham in London. So it came about that Douglas Head Marine Drive No. 1 has been preserved for posterity.

It certainly merits its continued existence, for one glance shows it to be a most unusual vehicle. The lower deck seating is of the cross-bench kind more generally favoured on single-deckers like those of the Manx Electric. Moreover, No. 1 is 'one sided' – that is, the entrances to both platforms are on the same side, while the two stairways are both on the opposite side. The reason for this is that for most of its way the line ran hard up against the face of the cliff, and passengers could only board the cars from one side. To complete its unusualness, No. 1 is of 4 ft. 8½ ins. gauge; although this is the standard gauge of tramways in Britain, it was very much non-standard for the Isle of Man, where the Douglas Head Marine Drive Tramway was the only line of this gauge. No. 1 was built in 1896 by Brush on a Lord Baltimore truck from the United States.

22 Glasgow 'Room-and-Kitchen'
The American influence that was noticeable in British electric tramcar design in its early days is detectable in Glasgow's 'Room-and-Kitchen' cars which were distinctly un-British in appearance. Bogie single-deckers with central entrance and an overall length of 34 ft., they were built by the Corporation for the opening of the city's first electric route in 1898. There were 21 of them, numbered 665 to 685, with equal-wheel bogies powered by two 35 h.p. motors. Total seating capacity was 50 in two saloons, hence the nickname. One of the saloons was for non-smokers and had fully-glazed windows, while the other saloon which was for the benefit of smokers had unglazed windows with blinds that could be drawn down to keep out the weather. The motorman had separate open-ended platforms. The popu-

larity of these strange vehicles was not such as to encourage the perpetuation of the design, and the Corporation soon came to the conclusion that the four-wheel double decker was better suited to the needs of the growing electric network. The 'Room-and-Kitchen' cars therefore had a fairly short life in normal passenger service, but one of them – No. 672 – was converted to a works car and still survives. In 1962 it was restored to its original condition to take part in the ceremonial procession to mark the closing of the city's tramways, and it now has a worthy place in the Glasgow Transport Museum.

23 The Fleetwood 'Rack' No. 2
Fleetwood 'Rack' No. 2 was one of ten similar cars (Nos. 1 to 10) built by Milnes in 1898 for the opening of the Blackpool and Fleetwood Tramroad. The tramroad, though running along the streets at each end of its route, was something quite different from the common or garden town tramway, and was one of the few systems in Britain which resembled the American 'interurban', which on reaching the fringe of the built-up area happily took to its own right-of-way and sped off across the countryside. The Blackpool and Fleetwood was like this, so it was hardly surprising that its rolling stock looked vaguely American. 'Rack' (short for 'toastrack' from the resemblance of its seating to the breakfast-table item) No. 2 has a long wheelbase suited to the spaciousness of the sleeper track rather than the cramped corners of the average town tramway. Moreover, its open type of body is more suited to the nature of the holiday traffic it carried on the line – in this connection its strong resemblance to the contemporary cross-bench cars of the Manx Electric will be noted, for both lines had much in common in their origins. No. 2 can seat 48 passengers, and has Milnes plate-frame bogies. The Blackpool and Fleetwood was taken over by Blackpool Corporation in 1920, and the pioneer

'Racks' were re-numbered 126 to 135. They were still to be seen in service as late as 1939, but after some of them had had their careers prolonged by being taken over by the works department, only one of them survived until 1960, when it was one of four veterans restored to mark the celebration of 75 years of the Blackpool tramways. It still exists to carry passengers at the Crich Museum – and of course you can still travel on the tramroad in a modern Blackpool Corporation car.

24   **Blackpool 'Dreadnought' No. 59**
Well might it be called a 'Dreadnought', for it must rank among the most fearsome-looking tramcars ever designed. With its full-width end steps and twin stairways, it looked as though it was capable of scooping up passengers by the score – as indeed it was; it had a seating capacity of 86 – 37 in the saloon and 49 on the open top deck. Not surprisingly, the 'Dreadnoughts' were just the thing for moving the holiday crowds along the Promenade. The class came on the scene in 1898, when Nos. 15 and 16 were delivered by Milnes. Ten more (Nos. 17 to 26) came in 1899, while Nos. 54 to 61 put in an appearance in 1902. The unusual entrance layout was the patent of J. Shrewsbury; designed for rapid loading and unloading, it set a new record, rarely surpassed, of providing a tram with four stairways. Officially they were the 'Shrewsbury-entrance' cars, but it was always as the 'Dreadnoughts' that they were known, and they continued in service until 1934–35 when they were superseded by new double-deck stream-liners. However, one car – No. 59 – escaped the breakers, and took on a new role as tool room in Copse Road depot. Here it remained until 1960, when with three other veterans (the Fleetwood 'Rack' and 'Box' and the 1885 car No. 1) it was restored to pristine state to take part in the 75th anniversary celebrations of Black-pool's tramways.

25   **Sheffield single decker No. 46**
When the Sheffield tramways closed in 1960, there was a ceremonial procession of suitably decorated cars, and anyone watching this colourful parade might have been surprised to see a smart little single-decker bearing the number 46. The older in-habitants would have had to search their memory to recall the time when Sheffield had operated single-deck, passenger-carrying cars. But, in fact, No. 46 had been there all the time, though it might not have been immediately obvious since it had been sporting a different number and doing a different job. For, prior to its beautification for the festivities, No. 46 had been No. 354 (and before *that*, it had also borne the numbers 275 and 97) and it had been employed in the necessary but unglamorous role of salt car and snow plough. It had been serving this purpose since 1920, and it was a happy inspira-tion that led to its restoration, for it had indeed been a passenger car with the number 46 when it had been supplied by Milnes in 1899 during the initial period of Sheffield's electric tramways. It is now in the Crich museum.

26   **Dundee cars Nos. 1-10**
The Dundee tramcars had an indefinable atmosphere of timelessness about them, as though they had somehow mastered the art of remaining forever in a more gracious age. Basically they were enclosed double-deckers typical of the golden age on numerous systems up and down Britain, yet many of the Dundee models not only had a long lineage but had undergone drastic transformation in the course of their careers. Who would have guessed, for example, that Nos. 1 to 10 had started off as bogie open toppers? When they were built by Dick Kerr in 1900 to commence running on Dundee's new electric routes, they had Brill 22E maximum-traction trucks, as well as open top decks without canopies. The tops were later enclosed, but the real metamorphosis came during

the years 1928 to 1932, when the Tramways Department undertook a sweeping programme of modernisation. As a result of this process Nos. 1 to 10 took the shape in which they were known from then until their demise in the middle of the 1950s. Their bodywork was reconstructed to an all-enclosed pattern, complete with canopies and vestibules, while their new EMB trucks incorporated air brakes and higher speed motors.

27, 28, 29 The Glasgow Standards

If ever any tramcars deserve to join the ranks of the immortals, the Glasgow Standards do. For some 60 years they dominated the Glasgow scene, faithfully providing those almost-legendary cheap fares for which the city's transport was famed. The Standards covered practically the whole span of electric tramways in Glasgow, for the prototypes were in operation at the start of electric traction in 1898, and Standards were still in evidence almost to the end – while renovated specimens took part in the closing procession in 1962.

In all, around a thousand Standards were built between 1898 and 1924; except for 80 supplied by the Gloucester Carriage and Wagon Company, they were all constructed by the Corporation Transport Department at the Coplawhill Works. Trucks were of the 21E pattern. However, although those who knew the Standards in their later years may have thought them immutable, such was not the case in earlier days, for during the course of their long lives they underwent considerable modification, so that cars built at different periods to different outlines were later entirely reconstructed and modernised to produce a basically uniform vehicle. The initial cars were of open top type, with short canopies and open platforms; then in 1904 came the first with covered tops, and in 1910 the first vestibuled cars appeared. As each innovation was introduced, so it was applied to earlier members

of the class to bring them up to date. Then in the years between 1928 and 1935 further extensive modernisation was undertaken; this involved completely enclosing the cars, and fitting them with 8 ft. wheelbase trucks with 60 h.p. motors. This brought the Standards to the final pattern in which they are remembered today.

Of the six preserved specimens, No. 22 represents the Standard in its open balcony condition as it appeared when built in 1922, while No. 812 (built in 1900 as an open topper) is in the final modernised state. These two cars are at the Crich Tramway Museum. The other preserved Standards are Nos. 779 and 1088 at the Glasgow Transport Museum, No. 585 at the Science Museum in London, and No. 488 in the Paris Transport Museum. These Standards also indicate another feature of the Glasgow trams, the different colours used on the upper deck sides to indicate different routes; the colours were yellow, red, blue, green and white, and the services were so arranged that (with a few exceptions) no two routes carrying the same colours ran along the same streets. These colours were, however, given up after the Second World War.

30, 31 The Hill of Howth cars

The Howth trams were rather reminiscent of the Duke of York's men, for they marched up the hill and when they got to the top they marched down again. The five-mile 5 ft. 3 ins.-gauge Howth tramway, the last electric tramway to operate in Ireland, described a horseshoe-shaped course up and around the famous Hill of Howth, a notable eminence a few miles from Dublin, and a ride around the Hill was a popular excursion with Dubliners. In keeping with the scenic character of the line, the double-deck cars had open tops – though a substantial barricade of rails and wire mesh prevented you from leaning over the side.

There were ten passenger cars. Nos. 1 to 8 were built for the opening of the tramway in 1901 by Brush, and they were fitted with maximum-traction trucks of the Brill 22E type. They had 30 seats on the lower deck and 37 on the upper. Nos. 9 and 10 were added in the following year; they were built by Milnes and they had Peckham trucks, again of maximum-traction type but with the motors mounted at the outer end of the truck. This latter feature rendered them prone to derailment, and they were generally brought into service only at the busiest times. Internally the layout of Nos. 9 and 10 was very unusual, for most of the seating was in the form of a back-to-back knifeboard running the length of the saloon; this was intended to give the passengers the best possible view of the passing scenery. These two vehicles were also distinguished in that throughout their lives they retained the original teak-brown livery of the owners of the line, the Great Northern Railway of Ireland, whereas Nos. 1 to 8 were repainted in blue during the 1930s. All ten cars survived until the tramway closed in 1959, and then they achieved something of a record, for no fewer than five of them have been preserved as museum pieces, together with the repair car No. 11.

32 Dublin Directors' car

Although the tramcar is normally a strictly utilitarian vehicle, intended to carry the maximum number of passengers with the minimum of embellishment, there have been a few examples which demonstrate that, given the chance, it can burgeon out into a much more ornate form. Of course, these rare lavishly-appointed vehicles were not for the use of the ordinary passenger in his daily travels; they were designed for special purposes such as party outings or the journeyings of august personages. One such example is the Ryde Pier car we have already met (see Plate No. 1); another is the Dublin Directors' car, which – as its name suggests – was specially built to transport the directors of the Dublin

United Tramways Company. Although it is basically a three-window open-top four wheeler much like many of its contemporaries, here the resemblance ends – for the Directors' car is perhaps the most luxurious and decorative car ever to run on any tramway in the British Isles.

It was constructed by the company in 1901, and was at first mounted on a Peckham Cantilever truck, though this was later replaced by the unusual Lorain Dupont truck. But it is in the furnishing that the outstanding distinction lies. Inside the saloon were comfortable armchairs, while the windows were curtained and the lamps were shaded by decorative covers. The quarter lights featured pictures of Dublin scenes, and to complete the amenities there was a wine cupboard for the refreshment of the distinguished travellers. The upper deck was equipped with 16 swivelling chairs, and highly decorative panelling and elaborate ironwork added to the charm of the vehicle. When not carrying directors it was occasionally used as an illuminated car, but it was eventually sold off and now exists in a lowlier capacity as a summer-house.

33 Southampton No. 45

Knifeboard upper-deck seating was generally confined to the earlier varieties of horse car and was not widely perpetuated into the electric era, so it was something of a surprise to find knifeboards still operating in Southampton until well into the post-1945 period. The longevity of this arrangement in Southampton was due to the existence of the medieval Bargate, which presented a problem to the Transport Department for many years – the low curve of the arch limited the height of tramcars which had to pass through it, and it was not until 1938 that this obstacle was finally circumnavigated when both tracks had been relaid to avoid the need to negotiate the Bargate. Though low-height covered cars were developed and widely used, a number of open toppers continued at work as late as 1948. One of these survivors was No. 45, originally built by Hurst Nelson in 1903, and subsequently rebuilt more than once but retaining its old-time character as well as its knifeboard. When it was almost on its way to the scrap heap it was saved by the Light Railway Transport League, and has acted as a stimulus to the museum movement which has since developed. After many vicissitudes No. 45 now holds an honoured place at the Crich Tramway Museum.

34   London 'snowbroom' No. 022

You only saw No. 022 at work when the snow began to fall. Then it would emerge from its resting place in the heart of the depot, to begin its trudge through the wintry streets in order to sweep the snow clear of the tracks by means of its revolving brooms. It was still allocated to this duty as late as 1952, when the final abandonment of the last of London's tramways made it redundant. It is now preserved as a museum piece. However, it had not always been confined to its snow-clearing task, for in its younger days it had been a normal passenger-carrying car. It started life in 1903 as No. 106, a member of the London County Council's B class, an open-top double decker with three-window body and reversed stairs. It was built by the Electric Railway and Tramway Carriage Works at Preston and was mounted on a Brill 21E truck. In most respects it was similar to many cars produced for numerous different undertakings around this time, except of course that it had no trolley pole, for the L.C.C. employed the underground conduit system of current collection with plough and plough carrier mounted on the truck. No. 106 was later given a covered top, but after 1920 it was withdrawn from passenger service and converted to a snowbroom.

35   Newcastle F class No. 102

Newcastle 102 is a great giant of a tram,

37 ft. 6 ins. long and with seats for 84 passengers (36 inside and 48 outside). There is something elemental, not only about its size but about its gaunt outline; with its open top deck and open ends, it is almost the basic skeleton of tramcar. Yet in its first incarnation it was even more basic, for the F class of which it is the sole surviving member began life in the form of open-sided single deckers, supplied by Hurst Nelson in 1901. Before they entered service, though, the Corporation decided that such exposed vehicles were not the most suitable for the bleak Northumbrian climate (though open top decks remained to test the hardihood of Tynesiders for many more years), so the bodies were reconstructed as double deckers with enclosed lower saloons. Numbered 89 to 110, the F class were to be seen in numerous different varieties during their long careers; here was one with a top cover, there another with balconies and vestibules, and somewhere else yet another with front exits. No. 102, however, which went into service in 1903, remained an open topper innocent of canopies and vestibules. It was still operational when the Newcastle system ceased in 1950, and it was subsequently saved as a museum exhibit. The equal-wheel trucks are of the Brill 27G type, originally with two motors apiece but later with only one.

36   Lowestoft No. 14

One of the more endearing characteristics of certain of the smaller British tramway undertakings was their tendency to retain their original rolling stock completely unchanged throughout the existence of the system. While this may have given the ordinary passenger an erroneous impression of the immutability of electrical equipment, it did allow the specialist an opportunity of sampling historic vehicles; and it also helped to ensure that a sprinkling of such vintage items survived to the present day. A case in point is Lowestoft No. 14. One of four similar cars supplied in 1904 by Milnes, No. 14 is a splendid specimen of the car-builders' art of this period. It continued to serve practically unmodified until the town gave up this form of transport in 1931, after which it spent the next 30 years in that wilderness of chicken runs and garden sheds to which so many superannuated tramcars have been consigned. But – unlike so many others – it was eventually rescued, and hard work by enthusiasts has now restored it to something like its original state to form a proud exhibit in the East Anglia Transport Museum at Carlton Colville, on the outskirts of its home town. A 48-seat, open-top double decker of 3 ft. 6 ins. gauge, No. 14 is notable for its reversed stairs, its curved-top windows and its high roof, and it is envisaged that its restoration will be completed with the fitting of a correct type of Milnes girder truck.

37 Cardiff water car No. 131

In the 'golden age' of tramways the water car performed a useful service in laying the dust and in clearing out the grooves of the rails in city streets when road surfaces were by no means dustless and when the horse was still numerous. The tramway water car was generally of strictly functional design, with a cylindrical tank surmounted by a trolley pole, and a driving platform at each end. Cardiff No. 131, however, is a rather more elaborate example, with a built-up box-type body with long partly-enclosed platforms. It was built by Brush in 1905 as a rail cleaner, and in 1920 it was further embellished to serve as a 'scrubber' for the purpose of smoothing out corrugations in the track. The final abandonment of the Cardiff tramways in 1950 ensured that it would find no further employment in its native city, but it was saved from destruction by enthusiasts, and after being stored away for several years it achieved in 1959 the distinction of being the first tramcar to reach the Crich Tramway Museum. Though it is perhaps ironical that such a

completely untypical vehicle should be the sole survivor of the Cardiff system, its very unusualness makes No. 131 a particularly valuable museum item.

38 Belfast No. 249

As a representative of the tramway heyday, Belfast No. 249 has much to commend it. The four-wheel truck, the three-window body, the open platforms, and the open top deck with decorative ironwork around it, were features you could have seen on almost any other system throughout the length and breadth of the British Isles in the early years of this century – and indeed for much longer in many places. Yet strangely enough there remains some mystery about the precise origins of Belfast 249. Though it was constructed by the Corporation in 1905, it was intended as a replacement of a former horse car which had been ravaged by fire, and it may be that parts of the older vehicle were incorporated into the new. The truck is a Brill 21E. No. 249 still saw service as a passenger car as late as 1948, but thereafter its duties were of a more 'backroom' nature, for it then became a works vehicle. However, it was due to this change in its duties that it owed its survival, for it was still in existence more or less in its original condition when the Belfast tramways closed in 1953, and as a unique period piece it was then ensured of a place in the city's transport museum. It was also the last car to remain in the old-style red livery, for in 1929 the new blue livery was adopted for new or rebuilt cars.

39 Johannesburg No. 60

At first glance it is rather ironical that when a British television company wanted to film a typical British tramcar they should choose one that has come all the way from South Africa. Yet a closer look at the vehicle in question reveals that this is not so strange after all. For Johannesburg No. 60 really does appear to be the sort of tram you would have found in many different towns in Britain some 50 or 60 years ago; with its unvestibuled platforms and open balconies, it has just the right kind of 'look' about it. And again this is not surprising, for No. 60 was built in Britain. It was one of a batch of a hundred constructed in 1905 by the United Electric Car Company at Preston; 20 of them had open-top decks, but the other 80 (including No. 60) had covered tops. They were shipped out to South Africa to begin electric operation on the Johannesburg system early in the following year.

They underwent some reconstruction between 1923 and 1932, this work involving additional pillars to make five-window saloons instead of the original three-window pattern, as well as sliding windows on the upper deck. However, they retained their original open ends. Thereafter they continued with their ranks gradually thinning, until by 1960 only two of them were still carrying passengers. One of the two, No. 20, was the official 'last car' when the Johannesburg tramways closed in 1961, and this was preserved in the city as a museum piece. The other, No. 60, came under the wing of the Tramcar Sponsorship Organisation, which arranged for it to be transported back to England. Late in 1964 the voyage was made and No. 60 reached the Crich museum. It was in 1965 that it became a 'film star' when it was disguised as a car of the Notts and Derbys Tramways for the purpose of taking part in a televised D. H. Lawrence story.

40 Leicester No. 76

In many towns the tramcar could be seen evolving over the years by a gradual 'do-it-yourself' process, whereby the original basic open-top unvestibuled double-decker of the turn of the century was transformed into a completely enclosed vehicle. Leicester 76 typifies this process. One of a batch of 40 built in 1904 by the United Electric Car Company at Preston,

on Brill 21E trucks of 6 ft. wheelbase, it originally had open top and unvestibuled platforms. Leicester had its first covered-top trams as early as 1905, and gradually other cars were given top covers until eventually the last open topper went out in 1927. With vestibuled platforms, too, the process was a gradual one, and this was not complete until 1934. For their final years, then, the members of the Leicester fleet presented a picture of the characteristic all-enclosed double-decker, while other improvements such as upholstered seats had been added to keep the fleet reasonably up to date. Such were the potentialities of the traditional tram, and it says much for the original workmanship that it was possible to keep the basic vehicle – albeit much rebuilt – in satisfactory operation for more than 40 years. The last Leicester trams ran in 1949, but No. 76 was taken out of service in 1947. It then did duty as a cricket pavilion until 1961, when it was rescued for the Crich museum. Here it was put on to a 21E truck obtained from Glasgow, and has now been restored to its original open-balcony unvestibuled state.

41 Prague No. 180

At first sight, Prague No. 180 might seem an odd one out in a British museum, for it is quite unlike the typical tramcar of these isles. Yet this very difference is instructive, for seen now at the Crich museum No. 180 emphasises the converging lines of development followed by British and Continental practice. While the double-decker held sway in Britain, its Continental counterpart was the single-decker, normally with ample standing space on the platforms and generally hauling one or more trailers. Nowadays Continental style favours the lengthy bogie car or the articulated vehicle, still single-deck but of much larger capacity. No. 180 therefore remains an interesting example of characteristic central European practice of the period, just as much as its contemporary double-deckers at Crich represent British practice.

Prague No. 180 was built in 1905 at the Ringhoffer works at Smichov, and its design was perpetuated over many years as a basic standard for the fleet of the Prague city system. Eventually displaced on its home rails by new tramcars in 1948, No. 180 then went to Olomouc. In 1967, CKD-Praha (the organisation into which the Smichov works has been absorbed, and still an important builder of tramcars) generously offered to present No. 180 to the Tramway Museum Society, and after the car had been lovingly restored to its original 1905 condition, it made an exciting journey to its new destination in 1968.

42 Glasgow 'cable car' (Mains Department car No. 1)

Trams have come in almost every conceivable shape and size, but you would have to go a long way to find another one quite like the Glasgow 'cable car'. In appearance it is a box-like vehicle, with open platforms and sliding doors to the 'box', but while other operators had similar enclosed vehicles for carrying stores, this Glasgow example looks as though it has grown upwards to the height of a conventional passenger-carrying double-decker. Further, at the end it boasts a hoist, supported on a sturdy arrangement of beams. This apparatus gives a clue to its purpose, for it was intended as a special vehicle for the laying of feeder cables for the Corporation's electric tramways, and the hoist was used in manoeuvring the cable drums. Officially 'Mains Department Car No. 1', it entered service in 1906, mounted on a 21E truck. It still found itself a niche as recently as 1949, when it was employed in the installation of cables for trolleybuses. Happily saved from oblivion and restored to its old brown livery, this unique No. 1 travelled south from Scotland and arrived at the Crich museum in 1965.

43 Llandudno and Colwyn Bay Electric Railway original single decker of 1907

There was nothing quite like the Llandudno and Colwyn Bay Electric Railway. In the two North Wales coastal resorts of Llandudno and Colwyn Bay it looked just like an ordinary street tramway, but between the two towns it forsook the roads and provided a delightful scenic ride across fields and up and down hills. To work its services when it first opened in 1907 it obtained a batch of 14 cars that were almost as distinctive as its route. Unlike the conventional British tram, they were long single-deckers that were vaguely reminiscent of the amphibious character of the American 'interurban'. The bodies were by the Midland Railway Carriage and Wagon Company, while the equal-wheel bogies, each with two 30 h.p. motors, were by Mountain and Gibson. Each car had seats for 42 passengers, and there were entrances on each side of each platform. Later rebuilding saw the platforms converted to more conventional style, while the two motors on each truck were replaced by a single motor of higher power. Most of the cars were taken out of service when the second-hand purchases began to come along from Accrington and Bournemouth in the 1930s, but two of them (Nos. 17 and 18) survived until the last days of the tramway in the middle of the 1950s.

44 Sheffield 'Preston' cars

Among all the standards and the domed roofs which made up practically the whole of the Sheffield fleet in the post-war period, there were a few cars which were odd ones out. Into this category came the 'Prestons', which although having a general outward affinity to the mainstream, yet were distinguishable by being smaller vehicles with four-window bodies instead of five-window. A total of 15 cars were built for the Corporation in 1907 by the United Electric Car Company of Preston (hence the name). Numbered 258 to 272, they had seats for 22 on the lower deck and 36 on the upper, and were on Mountain and Gibson radial trucks. Although the bodies had open balconies, they had vestibuled platforms – the first Sheffield trams to possess this feature. In later years the class were rebuilt with enclosed top decks, and they were also retrucked with Peckham P22 trucks of 8 ft. wheelbase. In 1937 they were renumbered 336 to 350. Some of the batch were scrapped in 1939, but the last few continued active until 1954. No. 342 is in store for the future North East Regional Open Air Museum, near Durham, while No. 349 was converted to a stores car in 1951 and was used until 1967 as a generating car at the Crich museum.

45, 46, 47 London Transport E/1

If one car had to be chosen to represent the typical London tram as most people remember it, then the most eligible candidate would surely be the E/1. Sheer weight of numbers would ensure it a place in history; totalling over a thousand vehicles of London County Council origin alone, to say nothing of the many similar ex-municipal cars which were absorbed into the London Passenger Transport Board's fleet in 1933 and classified E/1, there was no other class in Britain that was so prolific. (Its closest rival was the Glasgow Standard.) Faced with dense traffic over a wide area, the L.C.C. went in for big trams in a big way. Another feature of the E/1 was its longevity; the first of the class entered service in 1907, while many examples were still at work as late as 1951. Construction of E/1s for the L.C.C. went on until 1922, with the basic design unchanged, so much was it abreast of the times. When the open top deck was common in many cities, the L.C.C. adopted the enclosed top at an early date; it was shrewd business sense to make the upper deck available in all weathers. Hence all the E/1s had covered tops from the start,

and the only obvious external change they underwent in the course of their lengthy careers was the fitting of platform vestibules in the 1930s; until this time the Metropolitan Police would not sanction the fitting of driver's windscreens. Internal changes included the substitution of transverse for longitudinal seats on the lower deck; though this reduced the total seating capacity from 78 to 73 (27 on the lower deck and 46 on the upper), the result was the inducement of added comfort. All cars were fitted for working on the conduit system as well as the overhead; at first the plough carrier was mounted on one of the trucks, but it was later transferred to the underframe between the trucks.

The E/1 was developed from the earlier E class, and between 1907 and 1913 nearly 900 were constructed; bodywork was by Hurst Nelson and Brush, as well as of the L.C.C.'s own building, while trucks of the same maximum-traction pattern were supplied by Mountain and Gibson, Heenan and Froude, and Hurst Nelson. Numbers were 752 to 1426, and 1477 to 1676. Then between 1920 and 1922 came Nos. 1727 to 1851, supplied by Hurst Nelson and Brush. (The L.C.C. numbers remained unchanged when all London's tramways were merged into the L.P.T.B. in 1933.) A 'last fling' was in 1930, when Nos. 552 to 601 were added to the class; officially 'rebuilds', these were new English Electric bodies on trucks salvaged from the old single-deck Kingsway Subway cars. Standard E/1 fittings included magnetic track brakes, which added to their lively performance at a time when the hand brake was still widely employed elsewhere for service stops. The surviving E/1, No. 1025, dates from 1908 and is in the Clapham transport museum. Other members of the E/1 class came from the municipal fleets of Croydon, East Ham, West Ham and Walthamstow.

48 London Transport No. 290

At first glance No. 290 does not look like a

typical London tram; instead of being a massive all-enclosed bogie vehicle like the /1, it is a comparatively small four wheeler with open balconies. Yet it is no less deserving of a place as a representative of the vehicles operated at one time by the municipal undertakings in the crowded streets of East London. West Ham was the largest of these municipal operators, having a fleet of some 130 when it was absorbed into the giant London Passenger Transport Board in 1933. The ensuing conversion of routes to trolleybus rendered large numbers of cars redundant, and No. 90 remains as a lonely survivor of London's four wheelers. Originally No. 102 in the West Ham Corporation fleet, No. 290 was one of a batch of six (Nos. 101 to 106) built in 1910 by the United Electric Car Company on Peckham R7 radial trucks. At first they had six-window lower deck saloons, but these were rebuilt in 1922 to the present three-window layout. The six cars were renumbered by London Transport as Nos. 289 to 294, and our were withdrawn in the face of the trolleybus invasion in 1937, followed by 90 and its brother in 1938. No. 290 was saved by London Transport and remained for several years tucked away in the back of a depot, until it was eventually resurrected to take a place in the British Transport Museum at Clapham.

9   Leeds ex-Hull No. 132

If it is the enthusiast's dream to find that every tramcar is different from every other, then this dream probably came as near as possible to being realised with the Hull cars that went to Leeds. For it certainly seemed that there were no two alike. True, they shared a family resemblance – of genus all-enclosed four-wheeler, with a somewhat domed roof and slightly tapered ends. But when you looked closer and compared one with another, it appeared that each was very much an individual. This one had a four-window body, and that one a three-window body; this one had upholstered seats, and that one had wooden seats; this one had a 21E truck, that one a P22; this one had a plain dash, that one a match-boarded dash. And so it went on. The connoisseur would delight in the individual idiosyncracies of each one, and note how it varied in internal colour schemes, in ventilators, seats, window layout and suchlike. Nevertheless, these variegated vehicles were useful additions to the Leeds fleet at a time when rolling stock was at a premium. The first batch were bought in 1942 and took Leeds numbers 446 to 477; a further ten were purchased when the Hull system closed in 1945 and they took the numbers 478 to 487. They had originated in a variety of former open-balcony and open-platform designs, though they shared such features as magnetic track brakes, and railway-type windows that let down with a leather strap. One odd piece of work that the new owners had to do to them was retyring the wheels, for Hull used a peculiar kind of rail with a centre groove on which ran wheels with a centre flange on the tread. The survivor of the batch is now at Crich; it is ex-Hull No. 132, built in 1910 by the City of Hull Tramways on a 21EM truck. It had a Bellamy roof until the 1920s, and got a P22 truck about 1933–34.

Another item included in the sale to Leeds was a works car, which became Leeds No. 6. This bore the family resemblance to its passenger-carrying cousins, but it earns a niche in history as a rare example of a works vehicle being sold by one undertaking to another. In its new home, No. 6 outlived its passenger-carrying companions.

50   Grimsby and Immingham Great Central No. 14

The Grimsby and Immingham Electric Railway could have made a good claim for the title of Britain's most unusual tramway. It started out as a fairly conventional type of street tramway in the town of Grimsby, and then it left the roads and sped off across fields to reach the docks at Immingham. The visitor might have been surprised also to find the tramcars bearing the lion-and-wheel totem of British Railways, for this was one of the few instances of a railway-operated electric tramway. It was in fact built in 1912 by the Great Central Railway to give access to its new docks at Immingham. Appropriately enough the rolling stock was in keeping with the 'main line' tradition, for the cars were imposing single-deckers of a length that rivalled a full-scale railway carriage. A dozen of them were some 54 ft. long and included a luggage compartment in the middle. Eight of the cars were built by Brush between 1911 and 1913, and the same maker also produced four smaller versions. The Great Central themselves built the other four giants in their own railway workshops in 1915, and one of these, No. 14, still exists as a museum piece. The Grimsby and Immingham passed under the London and North Eastern Railway with the grouping, and then to British Railways after nationalisation; it closed in 1961.

51 Leeds 'Convert' cars

As their name implied, the 'Converts' had been converted. Conversion, of course, was not an uncommon practice among tramcars, many of which underwent drastic rebuilding during the course of lengthy lives, for it has always been a characteristic of the British tramcar that it has been sufficiently strongly constructed to endure not only many years of service but extensive modification. The Leeds 'Converts' started out as open-balcony cars, quantities of which were produced by the Kirkstall Road works of the city's transport department between 1913 and 1923 and given numbers between 283 and 369. It was during the thirties that many of them underwent their conversion, the most obvious part of which was the enclosing of the balconies. This move was not

entirely straightforward, since the roof was not quite as long as the rest of the body, with the result that the ends had to be given a slight taper and a sort of valance along the roof line. The net effect was not unpleasing, for apart from being an immediate distinguishing feature, it helped to impart a slightly modernistic curve to the otherwise angular outline. The effect was also strengthened by the fitting of platform doors. Internal work included the replacement of the reversed stairs by normal quarter-turn stairs. Most 'Converts' retained their 21E trucks, though some were given P22s and air brakes to become 'Beestons'. However not all the open balcony models were converted, and a few were still operational during and after the war in almost unaltered condition; one of these was No. 309.

52 The Fleetwood 'Box' No. 40

If you've visited the Manx Electric Railway, your first reaction to the Fleetwood 'Box' will be 'I've seen that before somewhere'. The angular ends and the corner entrances are the exact replicas of features on the M.E.R.'s enclosed cars. In both cases the vehicles are the bad-weather counterparts of the 'Racks' (which are also similar on both lines). Car No. 40 was one of four (numbered 38 to 41) supplied in 1914–15 to the Blackpool and Fleetwood Tramroad Company by the United Electric Car Company on Dick Kerr trucks of the Mountain and Gibson type. Similar to an earlier batch dating from the turn of the century, they were the last new cars obtained by the Tramroad Company before it was taken over in 1920 by Blackpool Corporation. The quartet were then renumbered 112 to 115. Former No. 40's passenger days came to an end in 1938 when it was allocated to the engineering department. After pursuing these humble duties for many years, in 1960 it became the newest of the four veterans to be restored on the occasion of the 75th

114

anniversary of Blackpool's electric tramways, when it once again sported its old company livery. It is now at the Crich Tramway Museum.

53 Llandudno and Colwyn Bay Electric Railway – ex-Bournemouth open-topper No. 6

The open-top double-decker was characteristic of most British tramways in their early days, but its unsuitability to the vagaries of the climate generally led to its being roofed. One environment in which the open-topper lingered, however, was the seaside, where it had its attractions for the holidaymaker on fine summer days – a tradition perpetuated with open-top buses nowadays. The Llandudno and Colwyn Bay double-deckers in fact served on two seaside systems, for their original home was Bournemouth; when this system closed, the L.C.B.E.R. in 1936 bought ten of the cars, which then became the mainstay of its service until it too closed in 1956. They had the advantage that not only were the tops suitable for fine weather patronage, but the saloons were adequate for the traffic that could be expected at the off-peak periods. On the L.C.B.E.R. the cars were numbered 6 to 15; No. 6 had been built by the United Electric Car Company in 1914, and the other nine were built by Brush between 1921 and 1926. All were on Brill 22E maximum-traction bogies, and all had seats for 30 on the lower deck and 36 on the upper. No. 6 was bought in 1956 by Mr. Alfred Richardson and donated by him to the British Transport Museum at Clapham.

54 Dundee Nos. 34 to 51

Nos. 34 to 51 were further examples of Dundee tramcars which had been transformed. As with Nos. 1 to 10 (see Plate No. 26), this had taken place in the course of the Department's modernisation programme during the years between 1928 and 1932, and again this took the form of a rebuilding to an outline that was familiar to those who saw them in the years from then until the middle fifties. Again the design was all enclosed, with technical improvements like air brakes and higher speed motors. Nos. 34 to 51, however, did not have such a long pedigree as their companions 1 to 10, for they had been built between the years 1916 and 1921. Originally in open-ended form, they had been constructed by Hurst Nelson on Brill 21E trucks of 6 ft. 6 ins. wheelbase.

55 Sheffield 'rocker panel' car

The 'rocker panel', with its corresponding waist panel and waist rail, formed a characteristic part of the design of the traditional British tram, with origins lost in the antiquity of horse-vehicle days when the lower section of the bodywork had to be set in to allow room for large wheels. So the Sheffield tramcars that were given that soubriquet were by no means unusual; what was unusual was that they were the last design of Sheffield tram to carry this feature, for later designs were distinguished by flush sides. What were to become known as the 'rocker panel' class made their appearance in 1918, and as many as 150 were built between then and 1927. Nos. 36 to 60 and 376 to 450 were constructed by Brush, while Nos. 451 to 500 were supplied by Cravens. In addition there were four experimental cars numbered 366 to 369 built by the Corporation. A peculiarity was the curvaceous 'bulge' in the lower part of the vestibule screens to give space for the brake handle.

56 Llandudno and Colwyn Bay Electric Railway ex-Accrington

Among the hard-working members of the fleet of the Llandudno and Colwyn Bay Electric Railway were five single-deckers obtained second hand from Accrington Corporation after that town ceased tramway operation in 1931–32. This quintet made their appearance as Accrington Nos. 28 to 30 in 1919, to be followed by Nos. 31 and 32 in 1920. Built by Brush on maximum-traction trucks, they had longitudinal seats for 40 passengers. When they got to Llandudno they were renumbered 1 to 5 respectively, replacing the company's original cars of those numbers. Nos. 2 and 5 entered service on their existing Brush trucks, after they had been regauged from Accrington's 4 ft. to the Llandudno and Colwyn Bay's 3 ft. 6 ins. Nos. 1, 3 and 4, on the other hand, were put on to Mountain and Gibson equal-wheel trucks taken from the cars they were replacing.

57 Sheffield ex-Bradford cars

Nearly all of Sheffield's trams shared a distinct family likeness, from the oldest to the youngest, but in the early post-war years there were a few 'strangers' in the house. These were the second hand vehicles which Sheffield had purchased during the war to help its hard-pressed system cope with the needs of industry. Yet while ex-Newcastle cars were quite drastically reconstructed to a form that made them a fairly passable imitation of the home-built product, the cars that were bought from Bradford always looked decidedly non-standard. Not only did the different livery make them stand out, but the angular ends were quite unlike those of any of the Sheffield vehicles and were in fact characteristically Bradfordian. Not that the cars were completely unchanged after they made their move; to begin with they had to be suitably adapted from Bradford's 4 ft. gauge to Sheffield's standard 4 ft. 8½ ins. Another change was made possible by this change of gauge. Bradford's trams had open balconies, since all-enclosed four wheelers were not permitted on the narrow gauge, but in their new home the migrants had their balconies covered in to give them an altered profile that hinted at what the Bradford 'look' could have been if restrictions had not been so severe. The ten were built in 1919 by English Electric on Brill 21E trucks,

and with the contraction of their native system they were transferred to Sheffield in 1943 to take fleet numbers 325 to 334. The introduction of the 'Roberts' streamliners in 1950 rendered them redundant, but one of them (No. 330) was given a further lease of life by having its top deck cut off and being converted to a rail grinder, in which form it went to the Crich museum in 1960.

58, 59 Paisley No. 68 (Glasgow No. 1068)

In its present open-top form you probably would not recognise Paisley No. 68 as you might have seen it during its later years in Glasgow, when to a casual glance it looked much like a Glasgow 'Standard'. In fact it is now back in basically its original condition, for it was constructed as an unvestibuled open-topper. It was one of five, numbered 68 to 72, supplied by Hurst Nelson to the Paisley District Tramways in 1919 – a late date for new open-toppers to see the light of day. In 1923 Paisley's tramways were taken over by the neighbouring Glasgow Corporation and this quintet were renumbered 1068 to 1072. In ensuing years they were thus caught up in the mainstream of Glasgow's modernisation programme; No. 1068, for example, had a top cover added in 1924, while in 1931 it had the rest of the top deck enclosed and the platforms vestibuled, at the same time receiving new equipment including a new Brill truck of 8 ft. wheelbase to replace its original 6 ft. 6 ins. Brill truck. To all intents and purposes it was now one of the city's standard cars, its most obvious distinguishing feature being its three-window lower saloon with the wide corner pillars. It was withdrawn in 1953, and preserved by the Scottish Tramway Museum Society. In 1960 it travelled south to the Crich museum, where in 1966–67 it was 'de-rebuilt' to bring it back as far as practicable to its primal state as Paisley No. 68.

60 Llandudno and Colwyn Bay Electric Railway 'toastrack'

For the bare minimum of tramcar it would have been hard to beat the 'toastracks' of the Llandudno and Colwyn Bay Electric Railway. With bodywork consisting of little more than rows of benches, the toastrack tram was at one time popular at a number of seaside resorts, where its skeletal appearance was an obvious eye-catcher as well as an attraction for a bright summer day when a breezy ride along the promenade was a pleasant diversion. The Llandudno and Colwyn Bay had four 'toastracks', which were numbered 19 to 22. They were supplied around 1920 by English Electric and were mounted on Mountain and Gibson type equal-wheel bogies. The bench seats could accommodate 60 passengers, a remarkably high figure for a narrow-gauge single-decker. The 'toastracks' continued in operation until the closing days of the line in 1956.

61 Gateshead single decker No. 52

No. 52 was one of the smallest cars in the fleet of the Gateshead and District Tramways Company, so it was probably appropriate that it should have spent most of its time working the shortest route, that to Teams. The Gateshead system closed in 1951, and thereafter No. 52 was grounded for several years in the back garden of an ex-tram driver before going to the Crich museum in 1960. No. 52 is quite unlike the typical British tram, for this variety of small single-decker was generally found only on the most lightly-loaded routes or those where such obstacles as low bridges precluded the use of the double-decker. In fact, due to low bridges the Gateshead fleet consisted largely of single-deckers, although most of them were large bogie vehicles which tended to dwarf No. 52. In its existing form No. 52 was produced in 1920, though it was a rebuild by the company of former No. 7, a Preston-built car obtained for the opening of the

electric system in 1901. It was mounted on a Brill 21E truck of 8 ft. wheelbase, and in its rebuilt form it has seating for 32 passengers.

62 Cheltenham No. 21

In pre-war days, when many systems were in the process of abandonment, it was not uncommon for pensioned-off tramcars to find new uses as country cottages, summer houses, garden sheds or chicken runs. Here they would remain as mute reminders of past glory, until most of them eventually disintegrated under the ravages of time and weather. In more recent years, however, the growing interest in tramcar preservation has resulted in the spotlight being turned on such specimens as have managed to survive their exposure in any recognisable form, and in a few cases – such was the solid workmanship put into their original construction – it has been possible to effect a rescue operation. An example is Cheltenham No. 21. In 1932, about a year after the 3 ft. 6 ins. gauge tramways of the Cheltenham District Light Railway ceased to operate, the body of No. 21 found its way to a market garden where it remained as a tool shed for some 30 years until it was rescued by enthusiasts who undertook the arduous task of restoring it to its original condition. It can now be seen at the Crich Tramway Museum. No. 21 was one of three cars (Nos. 21 to 23) delivered to Cheltenham in 1921 by English Electric, on Peckham Pendulum trucks with magnetic track brakes. Although open toppers (as with so many narrow-gauge undertakings), they were an advance on the company's earlier vehicles in that they were vestibuled and were equipped with transverse seating on the lower deck.

63, 64 Stockport all-enclosed cars

The visitor to Manchester in the latter years of the tramways might have been forgiven for jumping to the conclusion that the only type of tramcar in existence was the enormous bogie vehicle on maximum-traction trucks, for such was the standard design of Manchester Corporation (see Plate No. 69). But then suddenly this first impression would be dispelled by the appearance of a nimble little four wheeler that looked almost tiny by comparison. The livery was a similar red, but this four wheeler belonged to neighbouring Stockport Corporation, whose cars for many years ran on joint routes between the two areas. If you took this car to Stockport itself you found that this was the centre of a network of routes which the Corporation worked by a fleet consisting entirely of four wheelers. Some 50-odd of the Stockport fleet of 80 or so comprised all-enclosed vehicles, which might have been taken as the epitome of the characteristic British double-decker. They were traditional, with all the features that you would have expected to find; wooden body, rocker panel, waist rail, top lights, and indeed practically everything that identified the British tramcar in its heyday before such concepts as 'streamlining' were thought of. Yet this apparent conservatism should not have led you to expect the worst, for in fact the cars were smartly kept, and inside there were remarkably comfortable upholstered seats. The bodies, mostly of the four-window pattern, were constructed by Dick Kerr, Cravens, or by the Corporation themselves, whereas the trucks were either Cravens or Brill 21Es. Manual track brakes were fitted for negotiating the occasional steep hill that had to be encountered. Stockport's cars continued running until 1951.

65 Gateshead bogie single decker

The bogie single-deck tramcar was an institution on Tyneside for half a century. In its later form, as represented here by Gateshead and District Tramways No. 5 which stemmed from the company's modernisation programme of the 1920s, it was an all-enclosed vehicle with rear entrance and front exit. There was something almost Continental about the whole concept of the design, with its large standing capacity and with separate entrance and exit. In this case it was partly forced on the company by the existence of low bridges precluding the use of double-deckers, as well as by the need for large-capacity vehicles on the short but heavily-loaded routes that characterised the Gateshead system, but it was no less an outcome of the company's progressive policy that led it to adopt such methods of working. No. 5 is a member of a batch of cars built in the 1920s by the company itself on Brill 39E maximum-traction trucks. After closure of the Gateshead system in 1951, it was one of 19 cars sold to British Railways for service on the Grimsby and Immingham Electric Railway, where it became No. 20 and sported British Railways green livery and the lion and wheel totem. After the Grimsby and Immingham also closed in 1961, it was saved and eventually found its way to the Crich museum to be restored to the livery of its native town.

66 Southampton domed-roof car

Open-top knifeboard No. 45 (see illustration No. 33) exemplifies the problem set for the Southampton Tramways Department by the low narrow arch of the Bargate. How to produce a top-covered car that could negotiate this venerable monument presented a knotty question; top-covered cars had made their appearance as far back as 1917, but they were so high that they had to be restricted to routes which did not have to squeeze through the Bargate. The solution came a few years later, when in 1923 the Department's Portswood works produced the first all-enclosed double-decker of the design that was to be the hallmark of the Southampton system thereafter. The most obvious feature of No. 12 was its deep domed roof, carefully contoured to fit the arch with almost nothing to spare, but incidentally imparting a pleasing modernistic touch in an era when the flat roof was still the vogue.

Wheels of only 27 ins. diameter, together with low-height saloons, kept the overall height of No. 12 down to only 14 ft. 7 ins. – more than a foot lower than the ordinary covered toppers. Transverse seats were provided for 26 passengers on the lower deck and 44 on the upper, giving a total of 70 which compared favourably with the early knifeboards. The truck was a Brill 21 E of 8 ft. 6 ins. wheelbase. Such was the success of No. 12 that between then and 1932 some 50 more similar examples were added, mostly on P35 trucks. A few appeared with three-window lower saloons instead of four, while the later ones were distinguished by having curved flush sides to the lower deck. After the Southampton system closed in 1949, three dozen of the cars were bought by Leeds, where 11 of them, renumbered 290 to 300, saw further service.

67, 68 Blackpool Standards Nos. 40 and 49

Like the proverbial old soldiers, the Blackpool Standards never died, they just faded away. It was perhaps surprising that in Blackpool, where such drastic modernisation had taken place, these thoroughly traditional type cars should have lingered on so long. The first inroads into their domain came in the middle of the 1930s, with the arrival of the first of the Railcoaches, and their last major field of operation was on the Marton route where they were finally displaced by the 'Vambacs' around 1950, yet the remaining few continued to put in useful appearances at busy times right up to 1966. In these final years too they acquired an outstanding popularity among enthusiasts, who seemed to be constantly chartering them for special tours; their non-conformity to the modernity, together with their undefinable vintage character, ensured that these occasions attracted admiring crowds. Now, though the Standards no longer run along the breezy seafront, no fewer than four of them have been kept as museum pieces;

two of them (Nos. 144 and 48) have gone to American museums as examples of the traditional British double-decker, while the other two (Nos. 40 and 49) are at Crich.

The Standards can trace their origins back to the early years of the century, though many were built by the Corporation during the 1920s when earlier vehicles were rebuilt to a similar pattern. No. 49 was built by Blackpool in 1926, and it is now in the red livery representative of the early 1930s before the more familiar green was adopted. No. 40 was also built by the Corporation in 1926, though apparently it was officially a rebuild incorporating parts of an earlier vehicle; it was subsequently vestibuled but, unlike others of its class, it retained its open balconies. Both cars are 78 seaters and run on McGuire-pattern, equal-wheel trucks.

69 Manchester bogie cars

'Big city – big trams' seems to be a generally applicable dictum, not least in Manchester where the 78-seat bogie double-deckers were for long a *sine qua non* of the streets. Though similar cars were to be observed in many parts of the extensive network of tracks that spanned the towns of South Lancashire, there were none quite like the massive Mancunians, with their maximum-traction bogies, wrought iron work and coloured quarter-lights, to say nothing of the distinctive livery with its elaborate lining. The first totally-enclosed double-decker in the Manchester fleet appeared in 1920; built by English Electric to the specifications of the tramways department. It was followed by others, and then in 1924 came a new design, of which over 200 were constructed in the course of the next five years, about half of them again having bodies by English Electric. At the same time the department's Hyde Road works was rebuilding older cars to a similar pattern, a process which was so drastic as almost to result in completely new vehicles. Most of the trucks were of the special Manchester pattern. Internally the furnishings were rather spartan, with wooden seats on the upper decks, while braking still depended on the driver's strong right arm (although rheostatic braking was also installed), but these vehicles remained on the road virtually unchanged until the final abandonment in 1949.

It is perhaps ironical that the sole survivor of Manchester's electric tram fleet should be so completely untypical. As was the case in so many other places, the double-decker was dominant in Manchester, and there was only one route on which single-deckers were employed. Nevertheless this singular route achieved a marked degree of fame, for the 53 was noted for its multitude of sharp corners and for the fact that it almost succeeded in making a complete circle around the city. It was also notorious for the fact that it was plagued by a disproportionate number of low railway bridges, and this was the reason why its operation was confined to single-deckers. Moreover, though they were very much in the minority, these single-deckers made up for this by being thoroughly unusual. They were of the 'combination' type, with a saloon in the centre and with open benches at each end, a design which apparently originated in sunnier parts of the United States, hence the name of 'California'. The 53 route was replaced by motor buses in 1930, and after that most of the Californias disappeared into that limbo of garden shed and greenhouse that was the fate of many a discarded tramcar. Eventually No. 765 was disinterred and has since been undergoing restoration. It originated in Manchester Corporation's Hyde Road works in 1913, and ran on Brill 22E maximum-traction trucks.

70 **Bradford No. 104**

While No. 104 is entirely representative of the Bradford fleet in its later years, it also has two particular claims to fame. First, it was the city's official 'last car' in 1950, when it was suitably decorated to convey civic dignitaries on the final run. Second, although after these ceremonies it was sold off to act as a scorer's box at Odsal football stadium, it was later salvaged and restored to working order; moreover a length of track was also brought back into use so that 104 really had somewhere to show its paces.

The rescue operation involved not only bringing the body out of the stadium, but also finding a suitable truck (for the original had been scrapped). A 21E truck of the correct type was obtained from Sheffield and regauged to Bradford's 4 ft., while other missing items were dug out from odd corners to complete the job. The car was repainted in the dark blue livery that had been standard before the more familiar light blue had been adopted in 1942. When the work was complete No. 104 made its first journey in its restored form in 1958 along a length of track which had still survived and had now been specially cleaned out at the approach to the depot and works at Thornbury. The location was appropriate, since it was at Thornbury works that the department built most of the city's tramcars from 1912 to 1931. They were all basically the same as No. 104, which was turned out in 1925 on a 21E truck of 7 ft. wheelbase; it seated 19 on the lower deck and 43 on the upper. The open balconies which were a characteristic of all the cars were necessitated by Ministry of Transport regulations forbidding the operation of all-enclosed, four-wheel double-deckers on narrow gauge tracks.

71 **London Transport E/1 ex-West Ham**

Over a long period the dominant species of London tram was the E/1 class, an enclosed double-decker on maximum-traction bogies. The classification E/1, however, was something of an umbrella term that covered several different varieties; although all basically similar, they possessed numerous differences in detail, as well as boasting different origins. Bulking largest among them were, of course, the London County Council vehicles which first carried the classification; No. 1025 is the survivor (see Plate No. 45). But other members of the class came into the London Transport fold from the municipal operators who were taken over in 1933 – thus there were examples from West Ham, East Ham, Walthamstow and Croydon.

The West Ham specimens were constructed between 1925 and 1931. The first was No. 125, built by the Corporation in 1925, and followed soon after by another dozen numbered 126 to 137; of these Nos. 126 and 127 were again built by the Corporation, but the other ten were supplied by Brush. These 13 were renumbered 331 to 343 in the London Transport fleet. West Ham No. 138, of similar pattern, was built by the Corporation in 1928, and this was followed by Brush-built Nos. 69 to 74 and 76 to 85 in 1929–30; the missing No. 75 was another Corporation product of 1930. Under London Transport No. 138 became No. 344, and Nos. 69 to 85 became Nos. 296 to 312. The last addition was No. 68, constructed by the Corporation in 1931 and subsequently renumbered as London Transport No. 295. All were 69-seaters on Hurst Nelson-type trucks. When their native territory was claimed by trolleybuses they were transferred to still-intact southern routes, where most of them lasted until the dying days of the London system in 1952. Distinguishing points of these West Ham vehicles were the roller blind number indicators mounted above the destination indicators, and the beading around the top-deck sheeting which precluded the fixing of standard-size advertisements and so kept the upper-deck sides advertisement-free.

72 Aberdeen all-enclosed four wheelers Nos. 99–137

Although the final years of the Aberdeen tramways were dominated by the bogie streamliners, no less handy but more ubiquitous members of the fleet were the native all-enclosed four wheelers of more conventional aspect. Indeed these four wheelers were still giving good service in the closing days of the system in 1958. Their high-built construction lent them the ability to plough through the worst of the winter weather, while they were also responsible for operating the routes which the longer bogie vehicles could not negotiate. Woodside, for example, was exclusively a four-wheel preserve, due to the short passing loops at the city terminus. Yet if the bogie streamliners were impressive, these four wheelers were hardly less so. Though of the fairly traditional pattern, they had a character all their own, for they gave an impression of being immensely tall and dignified, an impression reinforced by the uncompromising angular ends. Representing the undertaking's first type of all-enclosed car, some three dozen dated from the years between 1925 and 1931, bearing numbers between 100 and 137. Many had bodies built in the Corporation's own workshops, but Nos. 106 to 115 and 126 to 137 had bodies supplied by Brush. The P35 truck was standard, though some had earlier been fitted with either 21E or E.M.B. Seating capacity was 64 or 66. There was no car bearing the number 125; the parts were obtained for this, but in the event they were used only as spares. Certain open-balcony models of earlier vintage were also reconstructed as all-enclosed vehicles of much the same design.

73, 74 The Leeds 'Pivotals'

At first glance the Leeds 'Pivotals' looked much like any other trams of the mid-twenties; they were all-enclosed, four-wheel double-deckers with the conventional heavy wooden body, equipped with longitudinal seats on the lower deck and wooden seats on the upper. It was when your gaze fell a little lower that the unique attribute of the Pivotals became apparent. For, as their name implied, they were mounted not on the normal species of four-wheel truck, but on the unusual pivotal trucks. These represented one of the numerous attempts over the years to create a four wheeler that would ride as well as a bogie car but without the expense and complication of bogies. The E.M.B. pivotal truck consisted of two separate frames, each with a pair of wheels, connected to the body by rollers and connected to each other by an arrangement of levers. The idea was that the two frames should be free to pivot (in a similar manner to bogies) in order to allow the two axles to accommodate themselves to curves in the track. Leeds was in fact the only system which made extensive use of this type of truck, and from 1944 onwards many of the Pivotals were retrucked with the more conventional P35 truck. However, for many years the Pivotals formed a large part of the Leeds fleet, for there were some 200 altogether. Nos. 1 to 75 had bodies by Brush, while Nos. 76 to 150 had English Electric bodies, all these being supplied in 1926 and 1927; in addition between 1925 and 1928 the Corporation built others bearing numbers between 394 and 445 (except 399 and 402). Seating was for 26 on the lower deck and 46 on the upper.

75 Glasgow single decker No. 1089

For the tramway enthusiast one of the sights of Glasgow was the appearance among the Clydebank rush-hour traffic of the unique bogie single decker No. 1089. With a seemingly unlimited appetite for absorbing shipyard workers into its capacious interior, it was rarely seen outside this duty, though it had originally been intended to compete with the motor bus on such lengthy routes as the reserved-track line to Airdrie. It was built by the Trans-

port Department in 1926, on Brill 77E1 equal-wheel trucks imported from America, and was known as 'Bailie Burt's car' after its designer. At first it had a front exit, but this was subsequently abandoned after rebuilding. The experimental 1089 did not proliferate, and later attention was concentrated on the more traditional double deckers. No. 1089 spent much of its time on the out-of-town Duntocher branch, but after this was abandoned in 1949 it took up the Clydebank duties on which it was to be familiar during the last years of its working life. It is now an exhibit in the Glasgow Transport Museum.

76, 77, 78 'Progress', 'Lifeboat' and 'Gondola'

Decorated and illuminated tramcars graced many towns at one time or another, usually to celebrate some national or civic occasion, but nowhere have they reached such heights as at Blackpool, where they form an integral part of the great autumn illuminations. Several splendid examples created in recent years are still on parade and are illustrated later in the book, but it is worth glancing at three from earlier years – 'Progress', 'Lifeboat' and 'Gondola'. The Lifeboat was built in 1926, making use of the truck and underframe of a four-wheel passenger car No. 40 that dated from 1901. It included sails outlined in lights, while further lights represented the sea. In the following year the Gondola was constructed, again on the basis of a 1901 car, this time former No. 28; it included a shapely prow and an awning with appropriate Venetian atmosphere. In 1949, Progress was added to this colourful fleet; its basis was one of the Fleetwood Racks (see Plate No. 23), No. 141, dating from 1898. Progress was made to resemble outwardly one of the modern double-deckers (see Plate No. 111) with its windows outlined in lights; its side displays were changed for each season, but they included such features as a reproduction in lights of the Tower and such slogans as 'Greetings to our visitors'. Progress was withdrawn in 1958, while the Lifeboat and the Gondola followed in 1961 and 1962 respectively when the new illuminated cars Tramnik One and the Santa Fé train (see Plates Nos. 139 and 140) took their places to maintain the tradition.

79 Blackpool illuminated Standards Nos. 158 and 159

Among Blackpool's illuminated trams it has always been the 'set pieces' such as the Lifeboat and Gondola (see Plates Nos. 77 and 78) that have made the greatest impact. But hardly less attractive, and no less significant in the Transport Department's business, were the two illuminated Standards Nos. 158 and 159. Bravely outlined in coloured lights, they were an outstanding attraction for the holiday traveller, while their large seating capacity (a total of 78) made them a useful economic proposition. Moreover, even in daylight hours, they still offered the novelty of something different to ride on. Members of the Standard class (see Plate No. 67) Nos. 158 and 159 were built by the Department in 1927 with open balconies, being later reconstructed as enclosed vehicles in conformity with others of the class. They were 'lit up' in 1959, when rows of lights were fitted along the sides and around the windows, together with illuminated stars at each end. In this colourful guise they carried passengers on tours of the illuminations, while at other times, minus their lamps, they filled in on other duties when necessary. They were eventually withdrawn in 1966; one was sold to the East Anglia Transport Museum, and the other (for spares) to Crich.

80 London E/1 ex-East Ham, ex-Walthamstow and ex-Croydon

Like their West Ham counterparts (see Plate No. 71) the East Ham cars also bore a strong family resemblance to the standard London County Council E/1s

(Plate No. 45), their most obvious distinguishing feature being the route number indicator, which was of the roller-blind type instead of the stencil. These 20 cars were originally East Ham Corporation Nos. 51 to 70, and represented the first occasion that this operator had ventured into the field of the bogie car. Built by Brush in 1927–28, they were mounted on the L.C.C. type of maximum-traction trucks. The bodies had seats for a total of 71 passengers, and, as was common at the time, the platforms were at first unvestibuled, although the top decks were completely enclosed. After the formation of the London Passenger Transport Board, the cars were renumbered 81 to 100, and with the conversion of their home routes to trolleybus operation they eventually found their way to the remaining routes south of the river. Here all of them continued to operate until 1952.

Again looking very much like the ordinary ex-London County Council E/1 the 'Walthamstows' could be distinguished by their large stencil-plate route-number boxes. They originated in two batches. The first consisted of 12 cars obtained by Walthamstow Corporation in 1927; numbered 53 to 64 (Nos. 63 and 64 became 51 and 52 in 1932) they were built by Hurst Nelson and were mounted on Hurst Nelson maximum-traction trucks. At first they had unvestibuled platforms, and vestibules were not fitted until after they had become part of the London Passenger Transport Board's fleet in 1933. Such was the success of this dozen cars that Walthamstow obtained a further eight of similar design in 1932; these, however, were built by Brush on Brush maximum-traction trucks, and they were vestibuled from the start. All the cars had seats for 27 on the lower deck and 42 on the upper. After takeover by the L.P.T.B. the total of 20 cars were renumbered 2042 to 2061. Again with conversion to trolleybuses taking place on their home routes, they migrated southward to serve on the surviving south London routes, on which they continued to run until 1952.

Further members of London's vast E/1 class originating from operators other than the London County Council were the ex-Croydon Corporation cars. Basically the same as the standard E/1 variety they were distinguishable by the circular hole in the plough carrier, as well as by the large route-number stencil boxes. However, unlike the other ex-municipal cars from East London boroughs, they were still working on their native metals until the post-war years, for the former Croydon Corporation routes from Streatham to Purley, as well as the Thornton Heath branch, continued in operation until 1951. Originally numbered 31 to 55 in the Croydon Corporation fleet, they were built in 1927–28 by Hurst Nelson on maximum-traction trucks, and like most of their contemporaries in the Metropolis they originally had unvestibuled platforms. Their seating capacity was 69. When they were incorporated into the fleet of the newly-formed London Passenger Transport Board in 1933, they were renumbered 375 to 399. With the abandonment of the Croydon routes in 1951, 23 of the cars (two having already been scrapped) were transferred to New Cross depot to work remaining routes for a few more months, but the last of them were withdrawn from service at the beginning of 1952.

81 Sheffield No. 189

No. 189 is representative of some 200 cars built for the Sheffield tramways between 1927 and 1936. Basically they were the traditional variety of British double-decker, but given an extremely neat appearance by the flush sides without the usual rocker panels, and by the curved glass of the end windows. The sharp corners encountered on the city's routes limited the fleet to four wheelers, and the standard cars had an overall length of 32 ft. 6 ins. As with the great majority of Sheffield's trams, most of the bodies were

built in the Transport Department's works at Queen's Road. Seating capacity was 24 on the lower deck and 37 on the upper; though the total was lower than was sometimes obtained with four wheelers elsewhere, Sheffield installed two-and-one seating on the upper deck, which made for greater comfort. Peckham Pendulum P22 trucks of 8 ft. 6 ins. wheelbase rode smoothly over the well-maintained tracks. Equipment included two 50 h.p. motors and air brakes, with B.T.H. controllers having a single handle to control both power and brakes. A well thought out feature of the design was the vertically-mounted track brake wheel which allowed more room on the platform than the normal horizontal type. Before the last of this fleet had appeared, the new livery incorporating a lighter blue had been adopted, but older cars retained their original livery throughout their lives. The first of the cars was appropriately No. 1, built by Cravens, and later numbers of the Corporation-built models ran from 2 to 35, 61 to 130, 156 to 230 and 243 to 248. In addition to these, Nos. 131 to 155 were built by Hills.

82 Ryde Pier tramway

The majority of visitors to the Isle of Wight were familiar with the tramway that ran parallel with the railway along Ryde Pier, and for those who wanted to get no further than the town of Ryde itself this was a convenient means of saving a long walk down the pier. Though the double-track tramway had a long history, dating back to 1864 and involving horse traction as well as electric power (the early days are recalled by No. 3 shown in illustration No. 1), it is probably in its last form when diesel vehicles were employed that it is best remembered. Electric operation was given up in 1927, when two Drewry-built, petrol-engined cars Nos. 1 and 2 were put into service, one on each line. For a time they were coupled to trailers inherited from the electric regime, but these were then displaced by new trailers of matching design, while there was also an open luggage truck attached at one end of the 'train'. The motor cars were driven from one end only, hauling their trailers towards the shore and pushing them seawards, and after an accident when one trailer was pushed into the buffers, a warning device was installed at the seaward end of the track to indicate to the driver when to shut off power for the terminus. The petrol engines were replaced by diesel in 1960–61, and the tramway was closed early in 1969.

83, 84 Glasgow 'Kilmarnock Bogie'

Imagine a cross between a Glasgow Standard and a London E/1 and you have the 'Kilmarnock Bogie'; still with the same angular ends and low-set headlamp of the Standard, but with a long four-window body mounted on maximum-traction trucks. The first bogie double-deckers to run in Glasgow, the Corporation itself built the prototype, No. 1090, on Hurst Nelson trucks. The result was so satisfactory that it was decided to have a batch of 50 more, but the Coplawhill works were so busy at the time that the work had to be put out to contractors. Accordingly, during 1927–28, Nos. 1091 to 1120 came from Hurst Nelson, Nos. 1121 to 1130 from R. Y. Pickering, and Nos. 1131 to 1140 from Brush. All were mounted on bogies supplied by Kilmarnock Engineering (hence the family name) and each car accommodated 68 passengers on upholstered seating. With one major exception, the fleet remained basically unchanged throughout their careers, and were long associated with the lengthy route 9 between Dalmuir West and Auchenshuggle. The one exception was No. 1100, which in 1941 was modified with streamlined ends that vaguely resembled those of the 'Coronation' type, and was fitted with remote control equipment.

85 Blackpool steeple-cab electric locomotive

Although the reserved tracks of the Blackpool and Fleetwood Tramroad do have much of the semblance of a railway, it nevertheless came as something of a surprise to find a locomotive hauling a train of coal wagons along the tramroad. Yet this was a sight that could have been witnessed for some 20 years up to 1949. At the tramroad depot on the outskirts of Fleetwood there was a track which made a connection with the railway, and it was from here that railway wagons could make their way along the tramroad's metals as far as Thornton Gate, at which point there were sidings serving a coal yard. In order to operate this unusual service, a neat little steeple-cab electric locomotive was obtained by Blackpool Corporation from English Electric in 1928. A four wheeler powered by two 57 h.p. motors, it was equipped with trolley pole and headlamp like a tram, and with buffers and three-link couplings like a railway engine. With the ending of the coal train service, the locomotive found its occupation gone; in ensuing years it had only sporadic employment, and eventually it went to the Crich museum in 1966.

86, 87 Birmingham trams

Most of the larger undertakings evolved tramcars that had a marked local 'look', but few were more differentiated than those of Birmingham. Partly this was due to Birmingham's narrow 3 ft. 6 ins. gauge, which made the cars appear tall and thin; partly it was due to the shape of the vestibule screens with their curved protuberances to accommodate the brake handles. Although, like other cities, Birmingham went in for the big bogie car on many routes, the fleet also included a large number of four wheelers which dated from an earlier generation. Their ranks were considerably thinned by the pre-war abandonments, but nevertheless many were still at work during the early post-war period. An example of these is No. 395, which still exists in the Birmingham Museum of Science and Industry. A typical four-window, open-balcony 3 ft. 6 ins.-gauge car, it is one of a hundred (Nos. 301 to 400) built in 1911–12 by the United Electric Car Company. Trucks were also by U.E.C. and were of 7 ft. 6 ins. wheelbase. In the lower saloon the wooden seats originally fitted were later replaced by upholstered.

Nos. 342 and 347 became odd ones out and earned a place as exceptions which proved the rule; for while the remainder of the type retained their open balconies throughout their lives, 342 and 347 had their balconies enclosed in 1921. Thus converted into all-enclosed vehicles, they appeared to be living contraventions of the Board of Trade safety regulation which laid down that no narrow-gauge, double-deck, four-wheel tramcar should have its top deck entirely covered in. In fact the Corporation had to obtain a special dispensation to carry out the work and to operate this pair in their new condition. However, no more of the four wheelers were so treated.

Bogie cars were distinguished by maximum-traction trucks of the 'Burnley' type, so called from their origin in that Lancashire town but finding much favour in this Midland city. Nos. 762 to 841 were distinguishable from earlier bogie vehicles by the fact that they had eight windows a side on the upper deck instead of four, though retaining the four windows a side on the lower deck. Built in 1928, they were the last new cars constructed for the Birmingham system, with the exception of the experimental cars 842 and 843. Nos. 762 to 811 were built by Brush on E.M.B. trucks. Nos. 812 to 841 were built by Short Brothers on Maley and Taunton trucks. All had air brakes to wheels and track, and had upholstered seating for 60 passengers. Nos. 762 to 811 were fitted with bow collectors for operation on the Washwood Heath and Alum Rock routes on which this

method of current collection was employed, though most Birmingham routes used the trolley pole.

The traditional tramcar was a massive vehicle, solidly made to endure a lifetime of pounding the city's streets. But although its heavy construction ensured its longevity it had the disadvantage that current consumption was high and speeds tended to be low, facts which were assuming greater significance during the 1920s when the influence of the swifter motor bus was making itself keenly felt. Hence the more perceptive tramwaymen were turning their attention to the potentialities of lightweight construction. One outcome of this was Birmingham No. 842, which was built in 1929. As a result of the extensive use of aluminium in the bodywork, the total weight of the car was kept down to 13 tons 12 cwt., compared with 16 tons 15 cwt. for one of the city's standard bogie cars. The body was built by Short Brothers and seated a total of 63 passengers – 27 inside and 36 outside. The Burnley maximum-traction trucks were powered by two 40 h.p. motors, and tests showed that current consumption amounted to a saving of some 17% compared with a 'heavyweight'. Air brakes were fitted, and the car was capable of a speed of almost 30 m.p.h. Its working life was spent on the Cotteridge route and it was withdrawn when this was abandoned in 1952. No. 842 remained unique, though another 'lightweight' appeared in the following year in the shape of No. 843.

If Birmingham No. 842 was a 'lightweight', No. 843 had even more of the surplus pounds trimmed off, for it turned the scales at only 12 tons 6 cwt. Like its companion, No. 843 made extensive use of light alloys, and its Duralumin bodywork, built by Brush, showed a saving in weight of some 2½ tons compared with a standard body. Furthermore, its trucks, which were of the Burnley maximum-traction type supplied by Maley and Taunton, had also undergone a process of redesigning which resulted in their weight being cut by about 2 tons. The two G.E.C. 40 h.p. motors enabled the loaded 843 to accelerate at a rate of $3\frac{1}{2}$ m.p.h. per second and to attain a speed of 27 miles an hour. Its equipment included air-wheel and air-track brakes, as well as magnetic track brakes. No. 843 was 33 ft. 6 ins. long, and though the limitations of the narrow gauge restricted its width to only 6 ft. 3 ins., it had upholstered seats for 60 passengers, 27 on the lower deck and 33 on the upper. It was constructed in 1930, and in appearance it maintained much of the established Birmingham 'look' of earlier cars in such features as the angular dash and vestibules, but its generally 'cleaned up' outlines were neatly topped by a domed roof. Intended as an experimental vehicle, No. 843 proved to be the last new tram for the Birmingham network, for thereafter the claims of the motor bus were predominant.

88 Blackpool Pantograph car No. 171

There was something definitely non-standard about the stately end-entrance saloons that glided along the Blackpool and Fleetwood Tramroad and then mysteriously disappeared off the Promenade into a side street to come to a full stop just outside Blackpool's North Station. They were clearly of a different generation from the streamliners that comprised the bulk of the fleet, and you were never likely to encountered them on any route but the tramroad from North Station to Fleetwood. Inside they were wide and spacious, with two and two transverse seating, that gave a satisfying air of solidity and almost a railway-like quality to the ride along the sleeper track. There were ten of the class in all (numbered 167 to 176) and they were built by English Electric in 1928. Their use of the pantograph current collector up to 1933 gave them the name by which they were generally known. Several were still in service until the end of the 1950s, while No. 174 received a new lease of life by being transformed into the coach of the 'Santa Fe Train' (see Plate No. 140). Meanwhile No. 167 had been handed over to the needs of the permanent way department, but when this role ended the car was given by the Corporation to the tramway museum at Crich, where it arrived in 1962.

89 Swansea and Mumbles Railway cars

Strictly not a tramway in the generally accepted sense of the term, the Swansea and Mumbles laid claim to being the first passenger railway in the world. Running a scenic course on its own right-of-way around the curve of Swansea Bay, the railway began carrying passengers as far back as 1807. Horse traction was employed at first, and then for many years steam locomotives were employed until electrification came in 1929. To work the new electric service the South Wales Transport Company introduced 11 of the largest electric tramway-type cars ever used in Britain. Each vehicle had a seating capacity of 106 – 48 in the lower saloon and 58 in the upper. Two further similar cars were added in 1930. All were built by Brush and had B.T.H. electrical and air-brake equipment, while a railway-like feature was the incorporation of a deadman's handle in the controller. Electro-magnetic contactor control was fitted, and the cars were equipped for working in multiple unit; at busy times they were coupled together in pairs to carry the crowds who flocked to the popular resort of the Mumbles at weekends and holidays. Apart from the outstanding size of these 45 ft.-long giants, their most unusual external characteristic was that both entrances to the car were on the same side, since passengers always boarded on the landward side of the line, which ran close to the sea for most of its five-mile route. The railway remained in operation until 1960.

90 Belfast Chamberlain car

When No. 342 came on the road in 1930, it was something of a giant among the Belfast trams, for with an overall length of 31 ft. 10 ins. it was longer than any other that had previously operated on the city's tracks. Moreover it was the first new car that had been added to the fleet for some ten years. Constructed to the specifications of the General Manager, William Chamberlain, No. 342 had seats for 68 passengers, 24 in the lower saloon and 44 in the upper, while an added touch of luxury was imparted by the installation of electric heaters in both saloons. The car was mounted on a Maley and Taunton swing-link truck of 8 ft. wheelbase, and equipped with air-wheel and air-track brakes, in addition to magnetic track brakes. It was the first of a batch of 50, numbered up to No. 391, of which the bodies of 40 were built by Brush while the bodies of the remaining ten were constructed locally by Service Motor Works. All were on Maley and Taunton trucks. They continued in service until the dying days of the system, always giving the impression of being the majestic grand dames among the lesser mortals, and they were the only type still operating at the time of closure in 1954. No. 357 of the class is now in the Belfast Transport Museum.

91 Dundee 'Lochee' cars Nos. 19–28

Although it was not all that rare to find a particular class of tram confined to one route on a system because of topographical limitations such as low bridges or other restricted clearances, few were so well known as to be commonly referred to by the name of the route they served. But into such a category came the 'Lochee' cars in Dundee. They were to be seen traversing a one-way loop that formed their town terminus and then climbing steeply up the hills to the north-west to reach the district of Lochee. Comparing them with other members of the Dundee fleet, you would find that the 'Lochees'

were wider; in fact, they had a maximum width of 7 ft. 2 ins., enough to permit them to be fitted with double transverse seats on the lower deck, the only Dundee cars in which this was practicable. It was this width that restricted them to their solitary route, for it was only on the line to Lochee that there was sufficient clearance to allow cars of such girth to pass each other, since the town's tracks were generally laid more closely together than the usual. The 'Lochees' were ten in number (Nos. 19 to 28) and they were the last new cars to be built for Dundee. They were constructed in 1930 by Brush on E.M.B. trucks of 8 ft. 6 ins. wheelbase and powered by two 60 h.p. motors. With an overall length of 31 ft. 6 ins., they had seats for 62 – 28 on the lower deck and 34 on the upper. They continued in service until the Lochee route was taken over by buses in 1956.

92 Sunderland No. 52, ex-Portsmouth No. 1

Portsmouth No. 1 was another unique vehicle that found its way second-hand into the Sunderland collection. No. 1 was the last new tram to appear in Portsmouth. Built by the Corporation on a modified Peckham cantilever truck of 8 ft. wheelbase, it was put into service in 1930. Its curved sides and domed roof gave it a smart aspect, while mechanically it incorporated such refinements as worm drive and air brakes. It had seats for 23 on the lower deck and 35 on the upper. With Portsmouth giving up tramways, No. 1 was sold in 1936 to Sunderland where it became No. 52. Alterations in its new home included the fitting of new stairways, which reduced the upper deck seating capacity to 30, and the replacement of the original truck by an E.M.B. in 1938. In 1940 the car was renumbered 45, and it was finally withdrawn in 1953.

93, 94 Manchester 'Pilcher'

Though officially dignified by such titles as 'Pullmans', Manchester's last new trams were generally known as 'Pilchers' after their designer, the Corporation Transport Department's General Manager, R. Stuart Pilcher. It was originally intended that 40 of these cars should be built, but in fact only 38 materialised and these were put into service between 1930 and 1932. Though retaining many of the features of the traditional Manchester tramcar, they were four wheelers and their aspect was improved by the curves of a domed roof. The bodies were built by the Department and each had upholstered seating for 22 passengers on the lower deck and 40 on the upper. The trucks were Peckham P35s of 8 ft. 6 ins. wheelbase, powered by 50 h.p. motors and fitted with magnetic track brakes. Fleet numbers were 104, 106, 121, 125, 131, 141, 144, 161, 163, 173, 176, 196, 217, 225, 228, 231, 242, 263, 266, 270, 272, 274, 287, 349, 370, 380, 381, 389, 420, 493, 502, 503, 510, 558, 610, 669, 671 and 676. With abandonment proceeding in Manchester, the Pilchers were offered for sale in 1946, and the whole class were despatched to four different new homes – something of a record; 14 of them went to Aberdeen (where they became Nos. 39 to 52), 11 went to Edinburgh (to become Nos. 401 to 411), seven to Leeds (Nos. 280 to 286), and the remaining six to Sunderland (Nos. 37 to 42). They gave several more years of service until the last of them were withdrawn in Leeds, Sunderland and Edinburgh in 1954, while the last of all survived in Aberdeen until 1956.

95   London Transport E/3

Perhaps the most famous haunt of the E/3s was the Kingsway Subway, where they could be glimpsed disappearing beneath the arches of Waterloo Bridge or roaring out of the darkness up the steep slope into Bloomsbury. Built by the London County Council Tramways in 1930 and 1931, the E/3s monopolised the Subway after it had been reconstructed to take double-deckers, and they were to be found on these routes until the tunnel was closed in 1952. After

this they spent their declining weeks on other routes until the final London closure later the same year. In general appearance the E/3 was a cleaned-up version of the stalwart E/1; it was an improved edition of the large bogie car so useful on the L.C.C.'s busy routes. Strictly speaking there should have been an E/2, but this apparently reached the drawing board stage in 1920 but never got beyond; hence the next in succession was the E/3. There were 150 E/3s altogether; Nos. 1904 to 2003 had Hurst Nelson bodies and initially were without vestibule screens. Nos. 161 to 210 had English Electric bodies, and were at first theoretically Leyton Council vehicles, though that authority's system was worked by the L.C.C. and the cars were numbered into the L.C.C. series. These Leyton cars had vestibules from the beginning. Upholstered seating accommodated 74 passengers; 28 in the lower saloon and 46 in the upper. Unlike the E/1s, the E/3s had metal bodies, a necessary safety requirement for working through the Subway; the bodies were flush sided, allowing slightly more room inside. As with the E/1s, maximum-traction trucks were fitted, this time by E.M.B., and again magnetic track brakes were standard.

96   London Transport HR/2

At first glance the HR/2 looked just like its contemporary the E/3, for their 74-seat metal bodies were of the same design. But if the distinctive 'ringing' of the HR/2's gears did not give it away, a look at its trucks did. For while most London tramcars had maximum-traction trucks, the HR/2 had equal-wheel trucks, each powered by two motors. The reason for this was that the HR/2 was designed to work the hilly routes (as the 'HR' of its designation indicated); on the way to Dulwich or Highgate, the gradients called for all axles to be motored, as well as for automatic run-back and slipper brakes. It was these massive E.M.B. bogies that gave the HR/2 its 'heavy' look, as well as its lively performance equally up hill as on the level, while another feature was the brake wheel on each platform to enable the track brakes to be applied manually. The HR/2s were built for the London County Council in two batches in 1930–31; Nos. 1853 to 1903 had bodies by English Electric and at first did not have vestibule screens, while Nos. 101 to 160 had Hurst Nelson bodies, vestibuled from the first, but with no trolley poles so that their scope was limited to routes working entirely on the conduit system. Three of the class (Nos. 1881, 1883 and 1886) were sold to Leeds in 1939, where they gave many more years of service, while the bulk of the class continued in their native city until the final days of the tramways. No. 1858 was saved by a local enthusiast, and after being exhibited for some time at Chessington Zoo in Surrey, it was moved to the East Anglia Transport Museum near Lowestoft, where it may now be seen.

97, 98 **The Feltham**

The Feltham is one of the classic tramcars. It upset the established conventions of some 30 years of tradition, and the concept of the tram was never quite the same again. The Feltham was seen in embryonic form in London streets during the mid-1920s, when the Metropolitan Electric Tramways and the London United Tramways produced experimental vehicles that were known under such names as 'Bluebell' and 'Poppy', but the first Felthams proper were put into operation in 1929 as M.E.T. Nos. 320 and 330. Their appearance was generally similar to the later models, their most obvious distinguishing mark being the lower cabs. Another experiment was No. 331, which had a central entrance and subsequently became Sunderland No. 100 (see Plate No. 99).

The outcome of these trials was the ordering of a total of 100 new cars, 54 for the M.E.T. and 46 for the L.U.T. They were built by the Union Construction

Company at Feltham in Middlesex (hence the generic name) and they were put into service in 1931. These production Felthams had rear entrances and front exits, separate raised motormen's cabs, straight staircases and an absence of internal bulkheads that imparted an air of spaciousness to the saloons. They had seats for 22 on the lower deck and 42 on the upper; this was a lower total than was usual on a bogie double-decker, but the seating was much more comfortable than the traditional, while the large vestibules allowed room for a load of about 20 standees. The cars were mounted on maximum-traction trucks constructed by E.M.B. and fitted with 60 h.p. motors, air brakes and roller bearings. The M.E.T. cars were numbered 319, 321 to 329, and 332 to 375; the L.U.T. cars 351 to 396. When the London Passenger Transport Board took over in 1933 the standard Felthams were renumbered 2066 to 2165 (M.E.T. No. 330 became 2167, and 331 became 2168).

With the impending closure of the London system, the 92 Felthams which had survived so far were bought in 1948 by Leeds, where they were transferred between 1949 and 1951 (though two of them were burnt out before they could make the journey). The 90 in Leeds were allocated the numbers 501 to 590, though half a dozen of them, in fact, did not enter active service in their new home. Others, though, were still at work when the Leeds system came to an end in 1959. Two of them survive, one in London and one in the United States.

99 **Experimental Feltham, Sunderland No. 100**

Bearing the highest number in the Sunderland fleet, No. 100 possessed a striking family resemblance to the Felthams in London and later in Leeds. The general outline and the raised cabs were much the same, but the outstanding difference lay in the central entrance. No. 100 started out as an experimental version of what were to become the famous Feltham fleets of the Metropolitan Electric Tramways and the London United Tramways (see Plate No. 97). It was built in 1930 by the Union Construction Company of Feltham and took its place as No. 331 with the M.E.T. With a seating capacity of 70, it had air-operated doors and was powered by four motors. It was destined to remain unique, since production models were built to the rear-entrance, front-exit design. After the formation of the London Passenger Transport Board in 1933, No. 331 was given the number 2168, but its days in its original home were limited; not only was it an odd one out, but the contraction of the London tramways meant that few routes remained that were worked entirely on the trolley system, and since its central-entrance construction made it impracticable to fit a conduit plough carrier in the usual position between the trucks, No. 2168 was offered for sale and arrived in Sunderland in 1937 to become No. 100. One of the unusual features of its internal furnishing was the use of longitudinal seating in the lower saloons; the seats were divided by arm rests in a manner reminiscent of a London Underground train. Like No. 99, No. 100 was not used during the war, and its term of active service ended in 1951. After much travelling, it eventually reached the Crich museum in 1961, where it is now being restored to M.E.T. livery.

Another experimental Feltham was London Transport No. 2167. It differed in having cabs that were in line with the rest of the lower deck instead of being in the raised position of the production models. Internally, too, there was another difference, for No. 2167 had reversed stairs; this was a reminder of its earliest days when it had been arranged for 'Pay As You Enter' operation, with the conductor sited at the entry to the lower saloon and the stairs accordingly laid out so that intending upper-deck passengers had to pass him and pay up. After a brief trial,

however, this method was quickly abandoned. No. 2167 was originally Metropolitan Electric Tramways No. 330, built in 1929 as one of the experimental vehicles that led up to the 100 standard Felthams. It was at first designed to take equal-wheel trucks and four-motor equipment, as had the experimental No. 320, but in fact it appeared with the maximum-traction bogies that were to become accepted Feltham practice. Renumbered as London Transport No. 2167, it later went to South London with the other Felthams, and was finally scrapped in 1949.

100   The Leeds Horsfield

'Neat' was perhaps the most appropriate epithet to describe the Leeds Horsfields (another example, by the way, of a car taking its commonly-used name from its designer). Though they were also widely known by the name of 'Showboats' (apparently after a popular musical entertainment at the time they made their debut), there was nothing at all showy about the design, which could claim to be among the neatest conventional four-wheel double-deckers so far produced. The straight sides, merging into the deep dashes with a stylish little curve, combined with the rounded end windows, showed what could be done with this traditional outline. The first of the class, No. 151, was built in the department's own works at Kirkstall Road in 1930. It had a level floor throughout the lower deck with no step into the saloon, quarter-turn stairs, and seats for 23 inside with 37 upstairs. Overall length was 31 ft. 6 ins. and width 6 ft. 11 ins. The truck was of 8 ft. 6 ins. wheelbase and had two 50 h.p. motors together with air brakes and magnetic track brakes. No. 151 was followed by three further examples built by the department using different trucks and equipments: these were Nos. 152, 153 and 154. Such was their success that it was very soon decided to order another hundred of similar design; these were constructed by Brush on P35 trucks, Nos. 155 to 204 having electrical equipment by B.T.H. and Nos. 205 to 254 by G.E.C. The installation of platform doors soon after the cars entered service further enhanced their appearance, while later modifications affected the upper-deck windows and the destination indicators. Most of the Horsfields operated until the final days of the system.

101 Sunderland ex-Huddersfield cars

The ex-Huddersfield cars in Sunderland could be immediately picked out by the fact that they did not sport the Corporation's standard 'streamline' style of painting on the dash. To the traveller they were also distinguished by the forward-facing front seats on the upper deck; these enabled you to enjoy the view forward while sitting the right way round, instead of having to sit sideways and twist your neck as you did on the conventional upper-deck end 'couches' on a tramcar. The 'Huddersfields' were another example of Sunderland Corporation's shrewd buys in the second hand market. Six of the cars were built in 1931 by English Electric on Maley and Taunton trucks of 8 ft. wheelbase and were numbered 137 to 142 in the Huddersfield Corporation fleet. Fully enclosed and with platform doors, they seated 20 on the lower deck and 42 on the upper. Two further cars were added in 1932 as Nos. 143 and 144. They were the last new trams built for Huddersfield, which in the course of conversion to trolleybus operation, offered them in 1938 to Sunderland, where they took the fleet numbers 29 to 36. Seven of them continued in service until tramway operation in Sunderland ceased in 1954.

102 Liverpool English Electric bogie cars

In their later years the Liverpool tramways were best known for the streamliners such as the 'Green Goddesses', but until the final days they could still parade numbers of the older-type four wheelers which had predominated until the early thirties. Many had been drastically rebuilt to make them more comparable with the advanced designs, but the rush hours could bring out a few without vestibules as late as 1949 while the odd one in the pre-1933 red livery could still be seen in 1951. Top covers of the Bellamy type (with no roofs over the canopies) appeared as early as 1902, but from 1921 came the more substantial top-covered car with roofed balconies and normal instead of reversed stairs, and generally mounted on a Brill truck. At first the balconies were open, but later examples had fully covered top decks and soon many earlier models were rebuilt in the same way. From 1928 on, new productions sported vestibule screens, and after that the all-enclosed vehicle was the norm and many of the older versions were correspondingly brought up to this standard. As they appeared during this period they were therefore all-enclosed cars of the species fairly characteristic of numerous systems, but they were marked by the unusual combination of a four-window top deck on a three-window lower saloon. Also outstanding were the large destination and number indicators which filled the ends from window to window.

A small batch of cars marked a transitional stage between these conventional four-wheelers and the full flowering of the modernisation programme of the middle and late 1930s. These were the 12 bogie cars – numbered 758 to 769 – built in 1931 and 1932 by the Transport Department using English Electric trucks of its own design. Developed for an experimental single-decker in 1929, these Priestly-designed trucks had inside frames and motors which formed an integral part of the truck. Each truck had a 60 h.p. motor mounted longitudinally and driving both axles. All but three of the dozen cars were later retrucked with more conventional E.M.B. lightweight bogies. The 70-seat bodies were fundamentally similar in outline to the contemporary four wheelers, though of course longer to suit the bogie wheelbase. Their obvious distinguishing feature initially was the long valance which almost hid the trucks. In 1933 a further dozen cars, numbered 770 to 781, appeared; they were of basically the same design, but they set the trend for the future in being the first to sport the new green livery instead of the red. They were mounted on E.M.B. heavyweight trucks.

103 Sunderland No. 86

No. 86 was a forerunner of modernisation in Sunderland, where by the early 1930s a new design was required for future development. Built in the Corporation Transport Department's own workshops in the short period of ten weeks, No. 86 made its debut in 1932 and was favourably received from the first. Its smart external appearance was graced by a new streamline style of painting, while the flush sides added to the impression of modernity. It was a 62-seater, with all seats fully upholstered. Mounted on an E.M.B. truck of 8 ft. 6 ins. wheelbase, it was powered by two 50 h.p. motors and had English Electric controllers and air brakes. It weighed 13 tons complete. Such was its appeal that within about a year it was followed by a dozen more of basically similar pattern; numbered 87 to 98, they were provided with more powerful motors. The bodies of nine of this batch were supplied by English Electric, while the remaining three were products of the Corporation's own workshops. The last of the dozen had the distinction of introducing the pantograph collector, which was to become standard in the town's fleet. No. 86 was the official 'last car' when the system closed in 1954.

104, 105 London No. 1

The smart double decker bearing the number 301 has been more familiar in recent years as a prominent exhibit in the Clapham Transport Museum, wearing the livery of the Leeds fleet in which it served from 1951 to 1957. But Londoners are likely to remember that before it went north it was an outstanding if elusive member of the capital's fleet, in which it remained a unique example of what might have been. As London County Council No. 1 it made its appearance in 1932 and was the last new tram to go into service in London.

In its general outline it bore some resemblance to the L.C.C.'s HR/2 class (see Plate No. 96), a resemblance that was reinforced by the presence of the equal-wheel E.M.B. bogies (though for the first time air brakes were fitted). But the similarity was little more than superficial, for in fact No. 1 heralded a breakaway from traditional patterns in many ways; not only was it smoother in outline, with all-enclosed ends instead of open vestibules, but it had platform doors, separate motorman's compartments and straight staircases, while the absence of bulkheads made the interior look remarkably light and spacious. Comfortably upholstered seats accommodated 28 on the lower deck and 38 on the upper; this was somewhat lower than on the conventional cars, but the standard of comfort was a good deal higher. Originally No. 1 was favoured with a royal blue livery – earning it the nickname of 'Bluebird' – and it was put to work on routes running through the Kingsway Subway.

With the formation of the London Passenger Transport Board in 1933, the design was not perpetuated and No. 1 remained an odd one out. After a few years it received the standard red livery and was generally to be glimpsed in rush hours only. When the contraction of the London system made it redundant, it went to Leeds to become No. 301, having been accepted in compensation for the two burnt-out Felthams. It eventually returned to its native city in 1957 to become a museum piece and a reminder of the direction in which London's tramcars might have evolved.

106 Leeds tower wagon No. 1

Most tramway undertakings possessed one or more works cars to do the odd jobs around the tracks, and most such vehicles dated from around the earliest days of the system and lasted until its end. In other cases 'new' works cars were created by the simple expedient of converting outdated passenger vehicles. It was rare for entirely new works cars to be constructed *ab initio* at any relatively late date, but one of the exceptions is the Leeds tower wagon which was built by the city's Transport Department as late as 1932. The need for its advent was also unusual, for it resulted from the extensions being made on the reserved tracks. The tower wagon was a vital accessory for any electric tramway employing overhead wires, but it generally took the form of a vehicle mounted on road-wheels so that it could be pushed aside and not obstruct the tracks when it was engaged on its attentions to the overhead. However, on the sleeper tracks of the reservations, where there was no road surface, such a vehicle was not practicable and a rail-mounted wagon was a necessity. Leeds No. 1 (it was initially No. 2) consists of a tower flanked by wooden cabs and mounted on a Peckham cantilever truck. It is lavishly equipped with two bow collectors, one above each cab. It is now preserved for the Crich museum.

107, 108 Dublin cars

The first thing that was likely to impress you about a Dublin tramcar was its great size. Somehow it always seemed so much more massive than its English counterpart. This impression was the result of a combination of two factors; first, the Irish gauge of 5 ft. 3 ins. not only made possible an extra few inches on the width of the car, but also enabled it to be somewhat broader in its lower parts and thus banish the tendency to top-heaviness that often manifested itself on narrower gauges.

Secondly, its design differed from the British norm in that the platforms, dashes and vestibules seemed to be an organic whole with the rest of the body instead of appearing as parts merely added on. Thus there was a clean line from end to end, terminating in vestibules that were more flat than round. Bogie cars were always in a minority in the fleet of the Dublin United Tramways, but in the post-war period you could be sure of seeing some on the long route to Dun Laoghaire and Dalkey, which had the distinction of being the city's first electric route as well as the last to be abandoned in 1949. The newest of the bogie cars dated from the earlier thirties, and were easily picked out by their domed roofs. Mounted on Hurst Nelson maximum-traction trucks with magnetic track brakes, they were built in the Dublin United's Inchicore works.

109 The Leeds 'Middleton Bogies'

Numerous individual types of tram have been associated with specific routes but few more so than the 'Middleton Bogies' in Leeds. Their route itself, with its track on private right-of-way climbing through the woods to a housing estate on a hill, was sufficiently out of the ordinary to warrant exceptional rolling stock and the Middleton Bogies were quite unlike any previous members of the Leeds fleet. The first of the class (No. 255) appeared in 1933. Built by Brush, its body seated 30 on the lower deck and 40 on the upper, and it was mounted on Maley and Taunton equal-wheel trucks. For the first time in Leeds, electro-pneumatic contactor control was installed, and the original controls also included regenerative equipment. The success of No. 255 was such that a further 16 were ordered and these came in 1935; all were on Maley and Taunton trucks, but while Nos. 256 to 263 had Brush bodies, the bodies of Nos. 264 to 271 were by English Electric. These 16 were basically similar to the prototype, but they were six inches shorter while inside they had the unusual feature that the stairways were on the opposite side from the normal. At first each car had two trolley poles, but these were soon displaced by the bow collector which became standard in Leeds after 1935. The field of operation of the 'Middletons' was extended in 1949 when their original route became a circular with the extension from Belle Isle, but they were only occasionally to be seen elsewhere. Most were withdrawn in 1955 and 1956, while the last of them, No. 268, ran until 1957.

110 The Blackpool Railcoaches

Blackpool went against the tide during the 1930s; when many towns were scrapping their trams, Blackpool was not merely retaining them but was putting into action a whole new and modern fleet. Though the newcomers were all of a generally similar style, there were four outwardly different patterns – there were single-deckers and there were double-deckers, and of both types there were open and closed versions. The double-deckers attained fame as the 'Balloons' (see Plate No. 111), while the open single-deckers became equally well known as the 'Boats' (see Plate No. 112). But the backbone of the new fleet were the enclosed single-deckers, the 'Railcoaches', of which there were several different varieties.

Precursor of this new fleet was No. 200, built by English Electric in 1933. Its central-entrance body was of composite construction and had seats for 52 – 24 in each of the two saloons, together with four tip-up seats in the vestibule. Overall length was 40 ft. The English Electric trucks were of 4 ft. wheelbase and were fitted with two 50 h.p. motors. No. 200 at first had a pantograph, but this was subsequently replaced by the standard trolley pole. In the next few months two dozen similar cars were put into service; these were Nos. 201 to 224. Another batch, numbered 264 to 283, were introduced in

1935. Then in 1937 came Nos. 284 to 303; of an improved design, these were built by Brush and had E.M.B. trucks. Finally in 1939 a further batch of English Electric cars arrived; numbered 10 to 20, these looked much the same as the others but were intended for operation during the summer only. For this reason they had windows which were permanently half open, as well as half-height doors and wooden seats. These cars became the 'Marton Vambacs' after the war (see Plate No. 126), while ten of the 1935 vehicles were later modified as towing cars to haul trailers (see Plate No. 136). Various alterations have been made to the range of Railcoaches during their lengthy careers and many still survive; in the 1968 renumbering, Nos. 224, 264 to 271, 282 and 283 became Nos. 610 to 620, while Nos. 284 to 300 and 302 became Nos. 621 to 638.

111 Blackpool 'Balloons'

Though the single-decker has long been ascendant in Blackpool it can still be literally overshadowed by the double-decker, for some two dozen streamlined 'Balloons' were obtained at the time of the modernisation of the mid-1930s. In general style they are clearly of the same family as the 'Railcoaches' (see Plate No. 110); they were built by English Electric in 1934–35 and were numbered 237 to 263. In fact they were initially of two very contrasting designs, for Nos. 237 to 249 at first had open top decks, the most modern examples of this characteristically British layout. These open toppers were intended to replace the 'Dreadnoughts' (see Plate No. 24) but while they symbolised the height of modernity in other respects, the popular open top was retained for the pleasure of holidaymakers on the seafront ride. The seating was for 40 on the lower deck and 54 on the upper, making a remarkable total of 94 that was fully able to match its predecessors. In bad weather the upper deck could be closed off from the lower by means of shutters at each of the stairways. During the war, however, the top decks were enclosed in order that the cars could be available for all-year use, with the result that they came to look much the same as Nos. 250 to 263 which were built as completely enclosed 84-seaters. On all the cars the trucks were by English Electric. In the 1968 re-numbering the Balloons were allocated the numbers 700 to 726.

Looking much like these Blackpool cars were two streamliners to be seen at Llandudno. The Llandudno and Colwyn Bay Electric Railway had two of these elegant vehicles, which it had obtained second-hand from Darwen Corporation. The most obvious difference from their Blackpool contemporaries was that they were narrower, in order to be accommodated on Darwen's 4 ft. gauge, and this meant that the seating was for two on one side of the gangway but only one on the other side; in consequence the total capacity was reduced to 24 on the lower deck and 32 on the upper. The two cars were built for Darwen in 1936 by English Electric and were mounted on English Electric maximum-traction trucks with 57 h.p. motors and air brakes. They were the last new trams obtained by Darwen, the rest of whose fleet comprised much more run-of-the-mill double-deckers, and when the Darwen system ceased operation in 1946 they went to the L.C.B.E.R. For this purpose the trucks were regauged to 3 ft. 6 ins. and the two cars were put into service on their new tracks in 1948. They were the first top-covered double-deckers the L.C.B.E.R. had ever had, and unfortunately the Ministry of Transport would not permit them to work over the more exposed sections of the line so that they were effectively limited to the operation of shuttle services at each end of the route. An odd point was that in the course of their transfer the two cars switched numbers. In Darwen they were numbered 23

and 24, but when they got to Llandudno No. 23 became No. 24 while No. 24 became No. 23.

112   The Blackpool 'Boats'

The basic tramcar design is capable of almost infinite variety, but certainly there had never before been anything quite like the Blackpool 'Boats' (though Grimsby's 'tram coach' was an earlier version of a similar idea). One glance at their pointed prows and low sides is sufficient to justify their nickname. In fact they bear a strong resemblance to the streamliners with which Blackpool was modernising its fleet in the middle of the 1930s, and they can be crudely described as single-deck 'Railcoaches' only waist-high (see Plate No. 110). For their own part in the modernisation plan they were intended as up-to-date replacements for the old toastrack cars which had for so long been popular for summer sightseeing tours. The Boats were 12 in number, Nos. 225 to 236, and they were built by English Electric in 1934 and 1935. They had English Electric trucks, with one motor apiece, and they had seats for 56 passengers. The central entrance was surmounted by a gantry carrying the trolley tower, which was of similar pattern to that used on the 'Rail-coaches'. In 1958–59 windscreens were fitted at either end to give the driver some protection, but otherwise he was as much exposed to the weather as his passengers. A familiar sight on fine days during the summer, eight of the Boats (Nos. 225 to 228, 230, 233, 235 and 236) were still operational in 1968 when they were re-numbered 600 to 607 respectively.

113   Liverpool 'Cabin' cars

The 'Cabin' cars got their name from the fact that they provided the motorman with the luxury of an enclosed compart-ment instead of simply making him stand on the platform. On the orthodox double-ended tram this was not so easy to arrange, since the platform had to be used in one direction or the other for loading, and overall dimensions generally left little room to spare for a separate driver's cab. The 'Cabins' also had platform doors, another item that contributed to the closed-in aspect, and again something that was not too common since it was usual for the platform entrance to remain open with nothing more than a chain or cord to shut it off from the street. Another unusual feature of the design of the 'Cabins' was the use of reversed stairs; these had been not uncommon in earlier days, but had now been widely superseded by the normal variety. The 'Cabins' were built in 1934 and were numbered 782 to 817; with one or two exceptions they were on E.M.B. heavyweight bogies. The smooth outline and domed roof hinted at what was to come in the later streamliners (see Plates Nos. 119 and 122). A basically similar batch of cars, numbered 818 to 867, was built in 1935 and 1936, but these had normal stairways and did not have either platform doors or segregated motormen's compartments.

114 Edinburgh Standard No. 35

The Edinburgh Standard fitted perfectly into its setting. Neat and dignified in design, yet with enough curves to look suitably up-to-date and aided by a sober yet stylish livery, it blended ideally with the historic streets of Scotland's capital. Basically a traditional four-wheel double-decker, the Standard also established something of a tradition itself, in that it remained in production substantially unchanged for a period of some 15 years. The first one – No. 69 – came out of the Transport Department's Shrubhill works towards the end of 1934, and from then until 1950 a total of 84 similar cars were produced. Because each one as it appeared took the number of an older car which it replaced, the numbering looks completely random, but the list is as follows: 1935 – Nos. 32, 55, 56, 62, 67, 71, 83, 88, 103, 105, 111, 112, 137, 145, 150, 157, 160, 164, 165,

189, 190, 202, 204, 229, 230, 269; 1936 – Nos. 45, 41, 120, 173, 195, 199, 232, 233, 234, 235, 236, 237; 1937 – Nos. 40, 82, 91, 238, 243, 247, 248; 1938 – Nos. 39, 63, 76, 218, 226; 1939 – Nos. 52, 215, 216, 220, 221, 222, 223, 227; 1940 – Nos. 54, 212, 214; 1941 – Nos. 72, 211; 1942 – No. 213; 1943 – No. 209; 1945 – No. 51; 1946 – Nos. 47, 66; 1947 – Nos. 59, 73, 210, 217, 224; 1948 – Nos. 35, 219, 228; 1949 – No. 37; 1950 – Nos. 48, 49, 50, 169, 172, 225. Peckham P22 trucks were used, and the seating was for 24 on the lower deck and 38 on the upper. No. 35, built in 1948, is now preserved in the Edinburgh Transport Museum.

115 The Belfast 'McCreary'

'The old "dog box" design has been totally ignored' – that was the comment of 'Transport World' on the smart appearance of the first Belfast 'McCreary' car when it made its debut in 1935. Certainly the 'McCrearies' demonstrated how far tramcar design by this period was adopting the smooth contours of the current vogue for streamlining, and they make an interesting comparison with the city's previous type, the Chamberlains (see Plate No. 90), introduced only five years earlier but of the traditional pattern. Again named after the reigning General Manager responsible for their design, the 'McCrearies' had curved ends, domed roofs and platform doors to complete their clean lines. There were 50 of the type in all, numbered 392 to 441. The bodies were of composite construction, and contracts for 20 of them were placed with English Electric while the contracts for the other 30 went to the Service Motor Works in Belfast on underframes by Hurst Nelson. Seating was for 24 on the lower deck and 40 on the upper. The trucks were supplied by Maley and Taunton, and were of 8 ft. wheelbase with two 50 h.p. motors and air brakes. As it turned out, the 'McCrearies' were the last new cars to be added to the Belfast fleet, for it was not long before the city was looking to the trolleybus for its future transport needs.

116 Sunderland Nos. 26 to 28

In 1935 Sunderland produced what may be described as its 'last fling' at a normal end-entrance tramcar, for interest was now concentrating on the central-entrance design of which No. 99 had already materialised. In such unorthodox company it was perhaps not surprising that Nos. 26 to 28 seemed to gather less than their share of the limelight, yet they were in themselves hardly less worthy of notice in representing the traditional double-decker in the pleasing shape to which it had evolved by the middle of the 1930s. Two unusual features were immediately apparent – the pantograph which had by this time been adopted as standard on the Sunderland system, and the twin head-lamps in place of the conventional single lamp. Curved glass in the roof added an especial lightness to the upper deck, while the 'streamline' paint style on the dash enhanced the modern 'look'. The bodies were built by the Corporation and were 32 ft. 9 ins. long overall, while they had seating for 28 on the lower deck and 36 on the upper. The trucks were by E.M.B. and were of 9 ft. wheelbase and powered by two 64 h.p. motors.

117 Sunderland central-entrance cars

No. 99 was odd man out. Not surprisingly, it caused quite a stir when it first took the road in 1934, for it was of a type hitherto unseen in the town. A large bogie double-decker with central entrances, it bore more than a passing resemblance to the modern cars then being placed in service in Blackpool (see Plate No. 111). It was built by English Electric, powered by two 57 h.p. motors, and was 38 ft. 6 ins. overall, with seats for 32 on the lower deck and 44 on the upper. Its smart, streamlined appearance with its twin headlamps helped

to break away from the conventional image of the tramcar and to give a pleasing air of modernity. Inside, two staircases permitted speedy movement of passengers, while the upper deck was made particularly light by the curved roof windows. No. 99 was doomed to remain unique in Sunderland, where it was almost the only bogie vehicle in a fleet of four wheelers serving the town's short but sharply-curved routes. It was out of action during the war, and then its post-war career was cut short when it was withdrawn in 1951. However, even though No. 99 did not multiply, many of the principal aspects of its design were perpetuated in the series of seven more central-entrance cars put into service between 1935 and 1940.

Unlike No. 99, though, they were all four-wheelers, the combination of a central-entrance body on a four-wheel truck having been made practicable by the introduction of a new design of truck by Maley and Taunton. In this, the truck side members were set in so as to leave room for the central entrance-way, while at the same time a channel section member took the place of the normal truck top bar. The first of the new cars – No. 55 – was supplied in 1935 by Brush on a Maley and Taunton truck of 9 ft. wheelbase. Brush also supplied the Corporation with the truck and body framing for another car, which was completed in 1936 as No. 54. Also in 1936 No. 53 was put into service; of similar design, this had an English Electric truck and framing by English Electric, while the vehicle itself was again completed by the Corporation. Four further cars of this pattern appeared later; Nos. 49, 50 and 51 were completed in 1938, while No. 52 did not enter service until 1940, making it the last new tram to be constructed for the Corporation's system. Yet another central-entrance four wheeler came as late as 1946, when Sunderland bought South Shields No. 52.

No. 52 was the last new tram to be added to the South Shields fleet, and it remained a unique specimen. Built in 1936 by English Electric, it was a central-entrance four wheeler that was obviously inspired by Sunderland's No. 55 which had appeared in the previous year and to which it bore a strong family resemblance. Externally, the most striking differences which marked it off from its neighbour's design lay in the arrangement of the saloon windows and in the single headlamp instead of the twin lamps. Internally it differed from the Sunderland example in that the central platform was slightly lower than the saloon floor, resulting in a 4½-inch step up into the saloon instead of a completely level floor throughout; in addition, the driver's cabins were somewhat larger, so that there was room for the driver to sit down at his work. Seating was for 60 passengers – 24 on the lower deck and 36 on the upper. Mechanically the car was mounted on the same type of specially designed Maley and Taunton truck, of 9 ft. wheelbase and powered by two 64 h.p. Crompton Parkinson motors. With the cessation of tramway operation in South Shields, No. 52 went in 1946 to join its cousins in Sunderland, where it took the number 48. It survived until 1954.

118 Sheffield domed-roof car

It came as something of a shock to see a Sheffield tram in green. The cream and blue livery, originally chosen to brighten the streets of the industrial city, had become so familiar that nothing else looked 'right'. Certainly the lighter paint was a challenge to keep in a clean condition, so it was perhaps not surprising that it should have been decided to experiment with another colour that would be easier to maintain. Hence in 1952 the green livery depicted here was launched, and a total of 23 cars were thus accoutred. However, this 'new look' failed to endear itself, and the cream-and-blue was accordingly retained. The car illustrated is one of the domed-roof type introduced in 1936 and

built up to 1939, during which time a total of 67 were constructed by the Department, numbered 231 to 242 and 249 to 303. Basically a development of the standard type introduced in 1927 (see Plate No. 81) they are another object lesson in what can be done with the traditional British four-wheel double-decker. The flush sides and dash, coupled with the domed roof and the neat window layout, combine to create a design that appears modern yet purely functional. The car is mounted on a Peckham P22 truck of 8 ft. 6 ins. wheelbase, and has seats for 24 in the lower saloon and 37 in the upper. One car of this type, No. 264, built in 1937, is preserved at Crich museum. During the war a further 14 vehicles of the same pattern were constructed to replace ones destroyed in the blitz.

119, 120 Liverpool 'Green Goddess'

The streamliners of 1936–37 were the apotheosis of the Liverpool bogie tram. Many bogie cars had appeared in the preceding years, when it had been decided that the city's tramways should be developed, but there were none quite like these. The old angularities had been replaced by smooth curves and pleasing lines that were to keep the cars looking pleasantly modern until their last days. Moreover, these cars did not come in odd ones or twos; in all there were 163 of them, one of the few instances of large-scale modernisation of that era. They were built in the Transport Department's Edge Lane works and were numbered 868 to 992 and 151 to 188. They seated 78 passengers – 34 on the lower deck and 44 on the upper – and one of the pleasing features was that the end seats on the upper deck were of the forward-facing type instead of the usual curved bench. Some cars had E.M.B. heavyweight trucks, others E.M.B. lightweights, and yet others Maley and Taunton trucks, but all had four motors and electro-pneumatic control. With the abandonment of the Liverpool tramways in the post-war years 46 of the Green Goddesses were bought by Glasgow, where they went into service between 1953 and 1956 after alterations that involved the replacement of trolley poles by bow collectors and the regauging of the trucks to Glasgow's 4 ft. 7¾ ins. They here took the numbers 1006–1016, 1018–1038, 1041–1049 and 1052–1056, but their size restricted them to certain routes and the last of them were withdrawn in 1960.

121 **Glasgow 'Coronation'**

Some tramcars have achieved a fame far beyond the confines of their native city, and there can be little doubt that high up in such a category come Glasgow's 'Coronations'. When they were introduced they were immediately recognised as setting a new standard for this mode of transport, and even today a look at one of the preserved specimens makes it hard for us to accept that this can possibly be a museum piece. The first prototype, No. 1141, appeared at the end of 1936, while the second prototype, No. 1142, came early in 1937 – Coronation year. No. 1142 differed from the first in having a five-window saloon instead of a four-window, and it was 1141 that was selected as the pattern for the production models when it was decided that a total of 150 should be introduced. Accordingly, Nos. 1143 to 1148 were built in 1937, Nos. 1149 to 1239 in 1938, Nos. 1240 to 1273 in 1939, Nos. 1274 to 1291 in 1940, and finally No. 1292 in 1941.

It had been intended that a further 700 'Coronations' should follow as replacements for older cars, but the war put paid to this plan; however, as late as 1954, half a dozen more 'Coronations', numbered 1393 to 1398, did appear, utilising trucks purchased second hand from Liverpool, and these were Glasgow's last new trams.

The 'Coronation' was 34 ft. 6 ins. long overall, and incorporated such features as platform doors and no internal bulkheads,

separate motormen's compartments, and curved roof lights. Remote contactor control was fitted, and the cars were mounted on E.M.B. lightweight trucks. They inaugurated a new livery of green, cream and orange, in place of the former livery which incorporated route colours, and accordingly they were the first Glasgow cars to make provision for showing a route number. 'Coronations' were still in service when the Glasgow tramways ceased in 1962.

122 **Liverpool 'Baby Grand'**

To all intents and purposes the 'Baby Grands' were four-wheel versions of the streamlined 'Green Goddesses' (see Plate No. 119). There were a hundred of them, numbered 201 to 300, and they were the last new tramcars built for Liverpool. All but two were constructed between 1938 and 1940, while the final two made their debut in 1942. All were on E.M.B. trucks. After the war they were extensively rehabilitated, with the result that they looked as good as new and exceedingly smart. In the final days the relative simplicity of their single-truck design made them more economical to maintain than the bogie Green Goddesses, and they were the last class to run in service on the Liverpool system. For the closing rites in 1957, one of their number, No. 293, was specially repainted and lettered as depicted here; it has since emigrated to an American museum.

123 **Aberdeen streamlined four wheelers Nos. 140 and 141**

Shortly before the war Aberdeen ordered four new tramcars of modern design; two were of the bogie type and two were four wheelers. It was intended that, before a larger order was placed, the two varieties should be tried in action to determine which was better suited to the Transport Department's requirements. The quartet were delivered in 1940, but wartime conditions prevented any more being btained for several years. When the order was at last placed, it was the bogie vehicles that were favoured, and the two four-wheel streamliners remained a solitary pair. Numbered 140 and 141, they were generally similar in style to their bogie brothers (see Plate No. 130), although with entrances at the ends instead of the centre. They were also of course shorter (at 31 ft. 6 ins.) and their seating capacity was correspondingly lower, totalling 64, with 28 on the lower deck and 36 on the upper. The upholstered seating of the upper deck was particularly attractive with its exclusive use of swingover transverse seats which provided a pleasant forward-facing seat at the front end. Folding doors were originally fitted to the platforms, but these were later replaced by roller shutters which gave an exotic touch to the doorway. Electrical equipment was again similar to that used on the bogie cars, with the exception of the motors, which were two of 57 h.p. fitted to the E.M.B. swing-axle truck of 8 ft. 6 ins. wheelbase. Nos. 140 and 141 were commonly to be observed on the Woodside route, on which short passing loops precluded the use of the bogie cars.

124 Glasgow experimentals Nos. 1001 to 1004 and 1006

Almost overwhelmed among the vast hordes of the Glasgow fleet, these five odd ones out can perhaps best be described as 'four-wheel Coronations'. Their fundamental styling was much like the more famous bogie 'Coronations' (see Plate No. 121), although of course they were shorter and their seating capacity was thus reduced to 60. Nos. 1001 to 1004 were built in 1940 in order to compare with their bogie compatriots from the point of view of operational economy for future vehicles, for at this time the question of a further fleet of new tramcars was still very much a live one. They were in fact lighter than the 'Coronations' and showed a favourable measure of economy compared with the heavier four-motor cars. One additional vehicle of the same basic pattern, No. 6, was built in 1943 to replace the Standard of the same number destroyed in the war in 1941, but later changes of policy meant that the breed was not perpetuated and the only post-war vehicles of new design were the bogie 'Cunarders' (see Plate No. 129). Nos 1001 and 1002 had Maley and Taunton trucks of 8 ft. 6 ins. wheelbase, while Nos. 1003 and 1004 had E.M.B. flexible-axle trucks, also of 8 ft. 6 ins. wheelbase. No. 6 inherited the Brill 8 ft. truck of its predecessor. An unusual item in the body styling was the sliding door to the platform.

125 Leeds 'Austerity' car No. 104

Although the Leeds network incorporated some well-laid-out reserved tracks, it also had its share of the more tortuous routes which bogie cars could not negotiate. The 'Middleton Bogie', for example, was specifically designed for the Middleton Light Railway on which it had plenty of room to spread itself, but it was barred from more congested areas. Hence, with the need for a modern variety of four wheeler which could go anywhere, the Transport Department in 1934 produced No. 272. With its domed roof and twin headlamps, it was described as of 'semi-streamlined' design. In fact it looked very much like a single-truck version of the 'Middleton', but it was distinguished by a decorative paint style ending in a large 'V' which earned it the sobriquet of 'Lance Corporal'. It was 31 ft. 6 ins. long, and had seats for 26 on the lower deck and 36 on the upper. The straight stairways were on the opposite side from the normal – that is, as you entered you immediately turned left to mount them. The intention of this arrangement, which also applied to the production batch of the Middletons, was that it would speed up loading and unloading, since the stairs led up direct from the entrance, leaving the platform clear to accommodate standing passengers. The truck was of the

Maley and Taunton swing-link type, with a wheelbase of 8 ft. 9 ins. and with two 50 h.p. motors. No. 272 was followed by two generally similar cars, numbered 273 and 274.

When No. 104 later appeared, it not unnaturally bore a considerable resemblance to the 'Lance Corporals'. No. 104 was the 'Austerity' car and it had something in common with the mythical phoenix; in 1942 Pivotal No. 104 was destroyed by fire, then in 1943 a new 104 arose to take its place. This new vehicle incorporated motors, gears, wheels and axles that had been salvaged from its unfortunate predecessor, while the rigours of wartime shortages compelled the Transport Department's workshops to exercise their ingenuity to create a complete entity under trying conditions. A thorough search in remote corners brought to light a quantity of second-hand wood suitable for the bodywork. The seating was also second-hand; for the upper deck, wooden seats salvaged from an old tram were employed, while the lower deck was more favoured in that, though the seating here was also reconditioned, it was of the upholstered variety. The truck, too, was second-hand, having been bought from the Llandudno and Colwyn Bay Electric Railway; a Brush P35, it had a wheelbase of 8 ft. 6 ins. Nevertheless, though necessarily the outcome of the contemporary custom of 'make do and mend', the finished product was quite presentable. It had an overall length of 31 ft. 3 ins. and a width of 7 ft. 1 in. with a seating capacity of 26 on the lower deck and 40 on the upper. Like 272–274, it had straight staircases situated on the nearside of the body. Its initial wartime livery immediately earned No. 104 the nickname of 'The Grey Lady', and it was not until the post-war era that it became No. 275.

126 **Blackpool's 'Marton Vambacs'**

Not unnaturally it is the seafront route at Blackpool that has usually received the most limelight, and the visitor might well have remained unaware of the existence of the Marton route. Pursuing a U-shaped course through the town – from Talbot Square through Marton and on to Lytham Road – it was admittedly less spectacular than the promenade track and savoured more of the normal kind of street route, yet in its latter years it was something of a model of modern tramway practice in Britain, for its frequent service was maintained by the smooth silent 'Marton Vambacs'. Numbered 10 to 21, these originated in 1939 as English Electric-built Railcoaches; though similar in outline to the other modern single-deckers with which Blackpool was re-equipping its system, Nos. 10 to 21 were designed for use in the summer peak periods only, and therefore had wooden seats and windows permanently half-open. They were reconstructed in more substantial and comfortable fashion during the war, and then after the war they were transformed into the Marton Vambacs.

This transformation had its genesis in 1946, when Railcoach No. 303 was experimentally put on to new Maley and Taunton HS44 trucks incorporating resilient wheels for silent running. These trucks were then transferred to No. 208, which was also provided with 'Vambac' (Variable Automatic Multinotch Braking and Acceleration Control) supplied by Crompton Parkinson. So impressive was the performance imparted by the new equipment that it was decided to fit it to Nos. 10 to 21; this was done between 1949 and 1952, this class becoming accordingly the 'Marton Vambacs', for they were employed almost exclusively on this route. In their renewed form they were immediately recognisable by the housing for the Vambac equipment at the base of the trolley tower, and by the inside-frame trucks. They continued on this duty until the Marton route was closed in 1962, after which they were scrapped, except for No. 11, which survives as a museum piece.

Sheffield Jubilee car No. 501

Sheffield's first new post-war tram, No. 501, was finished just in time to mark the celebration of the city tramways jubilee in 1946. Built in the department's own workshops, it was an obvious linear descendant of the compact four wheelers that had long characterised the fleet, but its outlines were somewhat more curvaceous. Its domed roof and rounded ends gave it a smooth modern look that was completed by the fitting of platform doors, while curved roof glasses added to the lightness of the upper deck. No. 501 was 32 ft. 6 ins. long, and had seats for 26 passengers in the lower saloon and 36 in the upper, in both cases extra spaciousness being given by the two-and-one seating. Upholstery was dominantly green in the lower saloon seats and maroon in the upper. The stairways were unusual in being of the half-turn type, instead of the quarter-turn that was standard on the city's cars. Night time found No. 501 particularly brilliant, for it claimed to be the first tramcar in Britain to be fitted with fluorescent lighting. The Maley and Taunton truck had a wheelbase of 9 ft., 5 ins. longer than any truck used on the fleet. It was powered by two 65 h.p. motors and had air-operated wheel and track brakes as well as magnetic track brakes. Thirty-five further cars of almost identical design (Nos. 502 to 536) were to follow in 1950–52 (see Plate No. 132).

128 **Leeds post-war double decker No. 276**

Making its appearance in 1948, No. 276 was Leeds' first new post-war tram and its last new double-decker. Built by the Transport Department in the Kirkstall Road works, it was 31 ft. 6 ins. in length and was mounted on a P35 truck incorporating two 50 h.p. motors. In general outline it owed much to the design of the 'Lance Corporals' Nos. 272–274 of 20 years earlier, but it was somewhat less streamlined and it lacked the 'chevron of

rank'. It also showed an affinity with the wartime 'Austerity' car No. 275 (previously No. 104 – see Plate No. 125), though it presented a rather smoother contour helped by rounded corners and recessed headlamps. Internally it incorporated the straight staircase that had become familiar on the earlier vehicles, while it had seats for 26 in the lower saloon and 36 on the upper deck. At the time there were hopes that No. 276 might have been the precursor of a whole batch of new vehicles, but in fact it remained unique and all later double-deck additions to the fleet were obtained second-hand.

129 **Glasgow 'Cunarder'**

It was appropriate that Glasgow's most modern design of tramcar should bear the name 'Cunarder' to symbolise the Clyde shipbuilding heritage, even if the more prosaic official title of 'Coronation Mark II' was more indicative of its lineage. In general appearance the 'Cunarders' looked much like the pre-war Coronations (see Plate No. 121), their most obvious external recognition points being the long guard rails covering the inside-framed Maley and Taunton trucks. One hundred Cunarders – numbered 1293 to 1392 – were constructed by the Corporation between 1948 and 1952; Nos. 1293 to 1297 in 1948, Nos. 1298 to 1316 in 1949, Nos. 1317 to 1369 in 1950, Nos. 1370 to 1391 in 1951, and finally No. 1392 in 1952. Most of them had seats for 30 on the lower deck and 40 on the upper. Four 36 h.p. motors were fitted, together with electro-pneumatic controls. Unfortunately the working lives of the Cunarders were fairly short, for soon tramway abandonment was under way in earnest; however, they were still well represented when operation finally ceased in 1962. Two of them survive; No. 1392 in London and No. 1297 at Crich.

A forerunner of the 'Cunarders' was No. 1005, known as the 'Blue Car' from the livery in which it made its debut in 1947 as Glasgow's first post-war tramcar. Apart from its colour, what gave it a unique quality was that it was a single-ender arranged with a front entrance and a rear exit. This arrangement was later reversed, making it reminiscent of the layout of the single-decker No. 1089 some 20 years previously, but finally its uniqueness vanished when it was converted to a normal double-ended rear entrance-exit layout in 1956. Moreover, in 1953 it had already lost its blue livery and adopted the conventional green, cream and orange. Initially No. 1005 had fixed seats for 36 passengers on each deck, folding doors at the front entrance, and a 'back up' controller on the rear platform for use when reversing into the depot and such-like manoeuvres. It was mounted on Maley and Taunton inside-framed bogies and had Crompton Parkinson Vambac controls. In its rebuilt form it had reversible seating for 30 on the lower deck and 40 on the upper.

130 **Aberdeen bogie streamliners**
With central entrance, folding doors and longitudinal seats, the Aberdeen streamliners had almost a Continental air about them. They were quite unlike the rest of the city's fleet, which otherwise consisted entirely of four wheelers, nearly all of them of conventional outline. The bogie cars were to be found on the busiest route, between Bridge of Dee and Bridge of Don, and were much in evidence in the dignified setting of the famous Union Street. The first of the cars, Nos. 138 and 139, were delivered by English Electric in 1940, at the same time as the two modern four wheelers which they much resembled (see Plate No. 123), but no more arrived until 1949 when there came the further batch of 20, numbered 19 to 38.

Very much like the earlier pair in appearance, they were built by R. Y. Pickering of Wishaw, sub-contractors to

English Electric. The bodies had an over all length of 38 ft. and an overall width o 7 ft. 1¾ ins. A single step from the centra entrance led to the two lower saloons, each of which seated 16 passengers, while a stairway each side of the platform gave access to the upper deck which had seats for 44 passengers. An attractive feature o the upper deck was the fitting of curved roof lights. The platform had folding doors and there were separate motormen' compartments, while an unusual embel-lishment was the installation of a public address system to enable the motorman to announce the stops. Electrical equipment was by English Electric and the trucks were of the E.M.B. lightweight type with four 38 h.p. motors. In 1952 the seating in the lower deck was changed from trans-verse to longitudinal, thus reducing the total seating capacity from 76 to 74 though allowing more room for standing. In 1954 further modification was under-taken when the doors were arranged for power operation to make it practicable for a car to be handled by one conductor instead of two as previously. With the final abandonment of the Aberdeen tram-ways in 1958, the bogie streamliners went to the scrap heap after a very short working life of only some nine years.

131 **Southend Pier Railway**
The vehicles of the Southend Pier Railway have been described as a cross between a London tube train and a Blackpool tram, and it would be hard to find a more apt description. The general outline, with twin headlamps, central entrance, and curved roof lights, recalls the Blackpool streamliners, while the seven-car trains with their air-operated sliding doors are distinctly reminiscent of the 'tube'. There are 28 cars in all, made up into four trains, each consisting of a motor car at each end and in the middle, separated by trailers. Placed into service in 1949, they were built by A.C. Cars of Thames Ditton, on resilient-wheel trucks supplied by Maley

nd Taunton. Each car is on a four-wheel
uck with the unusually long wheelbase
f 14 ft. 6 ins., made possible by the fact
aat the route is basically dead straight.
he cars are 29 ft. long overall and
ft. 6 ins. wide; seating is provided for 31
assengers in each motor car and 38 in
ach trailer. Rheostatic and air braking
 fitted, and current is collected from a
entre third rail. The present trains
eplaced the original electric stock which
ad been in operation since 1890–91 on
his 3 ft. 6 ins. gauge 1¼-mile-long pier
ailway.

32 **Sheffield 'Roberts' car No. 510**
he Sheffield 'Roberts' cars were not only
he last new trams to be placed in service
1 Sheffield; they represented the ultimate
1 that traditional British tramcar type,
he four-wheel double-decker. Basically
hey were of the same design as No. 501,
he Jubilee car of 1946 (see Plate No. 127),
he success of which inspired the order for
nother 35. Numbered 502 to 536, they
nade their debut in 1950, with deliveries
ontinuing until 1952, and they got their
ame from the fact that the bodies were
uilt by Charles Roberts of Wakefield.
Vith a total length of 32 ft., they had
eats for 26 on the lower deck and 36 on the
pper, the number being on the modest
ide through the normal Sheffield usage of
wo-and-one seating in spite of an overall
vidth of just on 7 ft. Exterior panelling
vas of aluminium, and other features
ncluded half-turn stairs and platform
oors. The trucks were of the Maley and
Taunton hornless type, with the long
vheelbase of 9 ft. as on the Jubilee, giving
teady running over the well-laid track
or which the Sheffield system was noted.
The two motors were each of 65 h.p. while
he controllers were by B.T.H., and air
nd magnetic brakes were fitted. In 1960
No. 510 was specially decorated for the
losing procession, and is shown here in
his embellished state in which it still
urvives at the Crich museum.

133 **Blackpool 'Coronations'**
     Nos. 641–664
With toastracks, boxes and railcoaches,
Blackpool had long established a 'single-
deck' tradition, so it was not surprising
that its new post-war fleet should also have
consisted of single-deckers. Delivered between 1952 and 1954, the 'Coronations'
were clearly of the same lineage as the
pre-war Railcoaches (see Plate No. 110)
with central entrance and streamlined
profile. However, not only were they
better – they were bigger; with a length of
50 ft., they were the longest trams ever
to run on the system. Further, with a
nominal width of 8 ft., they were not only
the widest in Blackpool but in the whole
country, and marked the first time that
this width had been reached with the
tramcar (though it was by now common
enough with buses). This had been made
possible by the fact that the 'main line'
of the Blackpool tramways was generally
spacious and free from sharp curves, and
by the fact that a far-sighted management
had for years been gradually relaying the
tracks at a suitable spacing to accommodate the wider vehicles. Mechanically the
Coronations incorporated the Crompton-
Parkinson Vambac equipment of the
kind installed earlier in the Marton
Vambacs (see Plate No. 126), together
with Maley and Taunton HS44 trucks
with rubber-insert wheels, resulting in a
suitably smooth and silent performance.
The bodies were built by Charles Roberts
and had sliding doors and fluorescent
lighting, with seats for 56 passengers. The
fleet of 25 cars was originally numbered
304 to 328; one car (No. 313) has since
been scrapped, but the other two dozen
were renumbered 641 to 664 in 1968.

134 **Leeds Nos. 601 and 602**
Not only were Nos. 601 and 602 completely unlike any trams that had ever
run in Leeds before, but their royal purple
livery, in honour of the Coronation year
of 1953 when they were introduced,

marked them out as something special. The bodies of the two cars were similar; built by Charles H. Roe of Leeds, they were central-entrance single-deckers with tapered ends, their overall length being almost 41 ft. 6 ins. Seats were provided for 34 passengers, and it was intended that a further 36 standing passengers should be accommodated, thus making an interesting comparison with the Continental practice of large-capacity single-deckers. However, though externally alike, the two Leeds vehicles were mechanically quite different. No. 601 had E.M.B. lightweight bogies and Metropolitan-Vickers electrical equipment, with four 50 h.p. motors. Rubber inserts in gear wheels and running wheels, as well as rubber mountings for the motors, reduced noise to a minimum. Air brakes and magnetic track brakes were fitted. The equipment of No. 602, on the other hand, was much less conventional; trucks and control equipment were of the American-originated P.C.C. type and were supplied by Crompton Parkinson. The inside-framed bogies each had two 45 h.p. motors driving through cardan shafts, while Vambac control equipment provided automatic acceleration. Braking was entirely electric; rheostatic braking slowed the car down to 5 m.p.h., after which solenoid brakes operated to bring it to a halt. Magnetic track brakes were also available for emergency use. On their first three days in service the two newcomers gave free rides to the public, who were duly impressed with the vehicles, but the design was not perpetuated and within six years the Leeds tramways were no more. No. 602 is preserved at the Crich museum.

135 Leeds No. 600

No. 600 was the last 'new' tramcar to be placed in service in Leeds. The term 'new' requires some qualification, since No. 600 was basically a rebuild, though in fact the finished product bore little resemblance to the original. It started its career in 1931

as No. 85 in the Sunderland Corporatio fleet, where it was an end-entrance single decker built by Brush and mounted o two Brush maximum-traction trucks. Sea ing capacity was 54. Intended for use o the Tatham Street route where a lo bridge confined the service to single deckers, No. 85 was withdrawn after th bridge had been reconstructed to allo double-deckers, and it therefore becam redundant in its home town. In 1944 was sold to Leeds City Transport, whe it disappeared into the workshops fo rebuilding. As the years went by, acquired the number 288 and its fina form became the subject of speculatio for it was not until 1954 that it eventuall made its debut as No. 600.

During this lengthy sojourn in Leeds had been completely transformed. It wa still a bogie single-decker, but it now had central-entrance layout, with new end incorporating separate motormen's com partments, and in general displaying more than passing likeness to the single deckers Nos. 601 and 602, whose design had helped to crystallise (see Plate No 134). Seats were provided for 34 passen gers, 17 in each of the two saloons, an again there was room for another 3 standing. No. 600 was mounted on E.M.B heavyweight trucks obtained second-han from Liverpool, while in the work of re building good use had been made of part and equipment from London, Liverpoo Southampton and Bradford. However, b this time the Leeds tramways were alread doomed, and No. 600, together with i two companions 601 and 602, gravitate to the short Hunslet route, on which th three single-deckers provided the basi service during their brief working lives No. 600 can be seen at the Crich museum

136 Blackpool prototype trailer se

To the onlooker the British tramcar ha been distinguished from its Continenta counterpart in two major ways: it ha normally been a double-decker instead of a ingle-decker, and it has normally travelled singly instead of in 'trains' of two or three. However, there are exceptions to every rule, and it is possible to point to numerous examples of British single-deckers. Less easy to find in Britain, though, has been the use of either coupled cars or motor-and-trailer sets. The London County Council did for several years employ trailers, while coupled cars were to be seen on the Potteries network, but the few instances here and elsewhere reflect the stringency of regulations which discountenanced the operation of anything more lengthy than a single car in the narrow streets of Britain's towns. Strangely enough, trailer operation – and with single-deckers moreover – is still to be witnessed on two of Britain's surviving systems, the Manx Electric Railway and the Blackpool tramways.

In Blackpool the present operation dates from 1958, when the first motor and trailer set was put into experimental working. This consisted of two of the 1935 Railcoaches (see Plate No. 110), one of which – No. 275 – had its motors and control equipment removed in order to act as a trailer behind No. 276. Special work included the fitting of automatic couplings and air brakes between the two vehicles. The result was a 96-seat unit more than 80 ft. long, and this was put into action on a special limited-stop tour of the coastal route between Blackpool and Fleetwood. Turning loops at the termini obviated the need for any shunting, while the railway-like nature of much of the line made the working of such a lengthy unit quite practicable. Its success was such that it was followed by the introduction of ten entirely new trailers (see Plate No. 138).

137   The 'Blackpool Belle'
When the 'Blackpool Belle' was launched for the autumn illuminations of 1959 it was obvious that the art of the decorated tramcar had reached a new high point. Probably never before had such an elabor-

ate and striking vehicle run on the tracks. Here is a wonderful replica of a Mississippi paddle boat, complete with the paraphernalia of gangways and lifeboats, and incorporating such ingenious devices as illuminated paddle wheels that really revolve and a 'sea' that really ripples! As many as 1,500 electric lamps are needed to supply all the effects and colours, while neat features of the Belle include the arrangement of the 'funnel' around the trolley standard. Seats are provided for a total of 36 passengers on benches on the 'deck' of the steamer; though the novelty of the ride made up for the somewhat exposed nature of the accommodation, this has since been glazed in. The overall length of the vessel is 45 ft., while it is 8 ft. wide and about 17 ft. in height. Underneath it all can be discovered the frame and bogies of former No. 163, which was an open toastrack of the kind that carried passengers on sightseeing tours along the promenade in the days before the streamliners arrived – but who could believe that now?

138   Blackpool trailers Nos. 681–690
Following the success of experiments with trailer operation in 1958 using modified cars 275 and 276 (see Plate No. 136), Blackpool decided to go ahead with ten entirely new trailers, to be hauled by suitably adapted motor cars of the 264–283 class. The new vehicles made their appearance in 1960 and took the numbers T1 to T10; in 1968 they were renumbered 681 to 690. The first new trailer trams for many a year, they were built by Metropolitan-Cammell Carriage and Wagon Company and were mounted on trucks supplied by Maley and Taunton. In general style the trailers matched the familiar look of the Blackpool single-deckers; they are 43 ft. 10 ins. in overall length and 7 ft. 6 ins. in width. In order to keep the weight down as much as possible, good use is made of aluminium and fibreglass in the construction of the

bodywork. Seats were provided for a total of 66 passengers. Automatic couplings are fitted at each end, together with hose connectors for the air brakes. When the trailer is coupled to its motor car, elastic cords are stretched between the two in order to deter passengers from attempting to walk between them. To haul the trailers single-deckers Nos. 272 to 281 (now Nos. 671 to 680) were suitably modified. Later alterations have included the installation of a driving compartment at the rear end of the trailer, so that the two-car set can operate equally well in either direction without having to be turned.

139 Blackpool 'Tramnik One'

In 1961 the Space Age came to the Blackpool tramways when 'Tramnik One' took off at the start of the autumn illuminations. The very first space rocket to be seen on any tramway, it was another triumph to arouse the 'Oohs!' and 'Aahs!' when it went into orbit along the Promenade. The rocket is, of course, rocket-shaped, with a pointed nose and a flared tail, and it is illuminated by some 3,000 bulbs. It has a row of windows along each side (perhaps not strictly in accord with the prototype, but then passengers want to see out) while it is mounted at an angle on its 'launching pad' as though about to blast off. The 'pad' itself consists of a platform which in reality hides an underframe mounted on a pair of bogies taken from Pantograph car No. 168 (see Plate No. 88). At the front, under the nose of the rocket, is the driver's cab. Passengers board via the tail, where two of the fins are cleverly arranged to accommodate steps and handrail, and a door leads into the saloon which has a rising floor so that the passengers at the front are at a higher level than those at the rear. Seats are provided for 46. To add to the illusion, passengers have a view at the front of the cabin of two 'astronauts' at an impressive 'control panel'.

140 The 'Santa Fé Train'

Blackpool's 'Santa Fé Train' is probably the most ambitious illuminated tram so far, for it is in fact two cars coupled together, with an overall length of no less than 90 ft. The 'locomotive and tender' were built up on the underframe and trucks of streamline single-decker No. 209, while the 'coach' consists of former Pantograph car No. 174 suitably doctored. The 'locomotive' is a replica of the American type of 4–4–0 that is almost a *sine qua non* in Wild West films, and is replete with enormous smoke stack, headlamp, bell and cowcatcher. The driver travels in the 'smokebox', while the 'tender' is fitted out to carry 35 passengers. The coach has seats for another 60, and has the attraction of open platforms enhanced with imitation wrought iron railings. A controller is provided on the rear platform for use when the 'train' has to run backwards. Sponsored by ABC Television, whose name appeared on the sides, the Santa Fé Train made its debut for the autumn illuminations of 1962. It incorporates well over 5,000 electric lamps, those on the locomotive wheels being so wired as to create the illusion of movement.

141 Blackpool's 'Hovertram'

With illuminated trams simulating such past and futuristic forms of transport as a Wild West train and a space rocket, Blackpool in 1963 added another up-to-date and topical example. The 'Hovertram' is a railed replica of that strange cross between aeroplane and ship, the hovercraft. With its low sleek lines, curved prow and roof-mounted engines, Hovertram really has the look of the original, while its aspect at night has the brilliance of 4,000 electric bulbs. The vehicle was sponsored by Shell, whose slogans are reproduced on it, and it was constructed in the Blackpool Transport Department's own workshops. Its basis is former Rail-coach No. 222, whose bogies and underframes it incorporates, but the bodywork is ntirely new. Passengers enter from the ack, to find a lower saloon with seats on ither side of a central gangway; a stairway n the off side leads to the upper deck, vhich has a side gangway. The lower eck can take 57 passengers and the upper 2, making an impressive total of 99; it is f interest to note, by the way, that the Iovertram is unusual, if not unique, for a louble-deck tram in seating more on the ower deck than the upper – in this case he upper deck is narrower than the lower n order to allow for the correct sloping utline of the prototype. Total length is 8 ft. The vehicle is single-ended, but ackward running is allowed for by a mall controller at the rear; this operates he main controller by remote control.

42 Eastbourne Electric Tramways No. 2

If you're building a new tram nowadays there is a lot to be said for making it look like a real vintage specimen, complete with open top deck and trimmings such as ornamental scrollwork. If your tram looks as though it may have been roaming the streets in the golden Edwardian era then it can hardly fail to emanate an aura of nostalgia that will be an irresistible attraction. So it is with Eastbourne No. 2, for though it entered service as recently as 1964, it very successfully captures the atmosphere of the London tramcar of the early 1900s. Its apparent prototypes were the early cars of the Metropolitan Electric Tramways and the London United Tramways which covered northern and western suburbs such as Finchley, Edgware, Ealing and Hounslow. No. 2 faithfully reproduces the open platforms, the headlamp above the short canopy, the staircase with its peculiar intermediate landing, and the top deck with its profusion of curly ironwork. However, No. 2 is no slavish copy, for it has a character all its own. Notable, of course, is its narrow gauge, which is the 2 ft. of the Eastbourne Electric Tramway which operated in the town's Princes

Park until 1969; notwithstanding, it is no toy, for it has a length of over 25 ft. and can carry as many as 35 passengers. Constructed in the operator's own workshop, No. 2 makes clever use of numerous components gleaned from former vehicles from Glasgow, Birmingham, London and Bournemouth, as well as from the Grimsby and Immingham Electric Railway and the Llandudno and Colwyn Bay Electric Railway. Now No. 2 is adding to its geographical versatility by moving to Seaton in Devon where the former Eastbourne tramway is being reconstructed.

143 Blackpool rebuilt No. 611

No. 611 is further proof that there is no answer to the question 'How long does a tram last?' For just when you might think that its days must be numbered, it can be renovated and restored so that it looks like new and is ready to start a fresh career. No. 611 was originally No. 264, and was built by English Electric in 1935 as one of the streamliners with which the Blackpool fleet was being modernised at this period (see Plate No. 110). Thirty years of hard work hauling holidaymakers up and down the promenade might have been thought a worthwhile return from the investment, but No. 264 was by no means ready to retire yet. In 1965 it disappeared into the works, and then early in the following year it reappeared in a new guise, so thoroughly refurbished that you might have taken it for a new vehicle altogether. Its original pointed ends had been replaced by a smoother design reminiscent of the 1952 cars (and incidentally adding another 18 ins. to its overall length); its sliding roof had been replaced by a fixed roof with flush-fitting curved roof lights to add to the neatness of the design; while shining aluminium panels at corners and beneath the doors enhanced its attractiveness. An innovation is the extensive use of plastic panelling for the exterior of the car; it is hoped that this will result in economy of maintenance as well as retaining its pristine gloss for a longer period. Now No. 611 looks fit for another 30 years.

144 'H.M.S. Blackpool'

For a seaside town what could be more appropriate than a ship as the prototype for an illuminated tramcar? And for the town of Blackpool in particular what could be more appropriate than a tram that really looks like the warship bearing that name. 'H.M.S. Blackpool' (the railed replica, that is) was launched for the illuminations of 1965, and like its predecessors it was a product of the Transport Department's workshops. Like the 'Santa Fé Train' and the 'Hovertram' (see Plates Nos. 140 and 141) it had a commercial sponsor, this time the Prudential Assurance Company. The basis of the 'ship' is former Pantograph car No. 170 (see Plate No. 88) whose bogies and underframe are utilised to carry a body that is 54 ft. long – the longest member of Blackpool's fleet. Passengers enter the warship from the rear (or should it be 'stern'?) to reach a saloon that has former bus seats for 70, and they can see out through eight large 'portholes' on each side. The driver occupies a separate cabin sited well forward. The imposing superstructure includes all the appropriate garnishings, such as guns, searchlights, funnel, masts and rigging, strung where suitable with coloured lights. The 'radar scanner' revolves realistically, while the 'crow's nest' conceals the base of the trolley pole.

145 Eastbourne No. 12

To design and construct a smart-looking modernistic single-deck tram is no mean achievement; to do this on a gauge as narrow as 2 ft. is a remarkable feat. No. 12 went into service at Eastbourne in 1966 to offer an added inducement to potential riders when inclement weather made the line's open toppers less patronised. And there can be little doubt that the enclosed saloon has quite a cosy atmosphere when the sea breezes are blowing. Not that the car is all that small; certainly it is under 5 ft. wide, but its length is no less than 31 ft. 6 ins. – equal to that of many standard-gauge four wheelers. Its seating capacity, moreover, is as high as 20; not on wooden benches or anything crude like that, but on real upholstered reversible seats situated on either side of the central gangway. No. 12 was constructed by the operators in their own workshop, with a body framed in wood and panelled in aluminium, and mounted on their own design of equal-wheel bogies. Ingenious use has been made of equipment purchased from other tramways, and the expert may be able to distinguish items from Leeds, Llandudno, Glasgow, Sheffield and Blackpool.

LIST OF MUSEUM TRAMCARS
IN DATE ORDER

For this list of preserved tramcars I am indebted to Mr. J. H. Price. The abbreviations are as follows: T.M.S. – Tramway Museum Society; B.R.B. – British Railways Board; A.M.T.U.I.R. – Association pour la Musée des Transports Urbains, Interurbains et Ruraux, Paris; M.T.M.S. – Manchester Transport Museum Society. An asterisk indicates that the car is not currently on display to the public. The list excludes certain surviving car bodies on which no restoration work has yet been carried out.

	Date Built	Owner	Location
I Horse tramcars			
Ryde Pier No. 3	1867	Hull Corporation	Hull Transport Museum, High Street, Kingston-upon-Hull, Yorks.
Oporto No. 9	1873	T.M.S.	Crich Tramway Museum, Crich, near Matlock, Derbyshire.
Sheffield No. 15	1874	T.M.S.	Crich Tramway Museum
Douglas No. 14	1883	B.R.B.	Museum of British Transport, Triangle Place, Clapham, London, S.W.4
Fintona tram No. 381	1883	Belfast Corporation	Belfast Transport Museum, Witham Street, Belfast 4, N. Ireland
*North Metropolitan No. 39 (parts)	?	39 Group	Woolwich
Aberdeen No. 1	c. 1889	Aberdeen Corporation	Edinburgh Municipal Transport Museum, Shrubhill Works, Edinburgh, 7
Belfast No. 118	c. 1890	Belfast Corporation	Belfast Transport Museum
Portsmouth No. 84 (rebuilt as electric car 1904)	1891	Portsmouth Corporation	North End depot, Portsmouth
Glasgow No. 543	1894	Glasgow Corporation	Glasgow Transport Museum, 25 Albert Drive, Glasgow, S.1
Chesterfield No. 8	1897	B.R.B.	Museum of British Transport, Clapham
*Swansea and Mumbles replica horse car	1954	B.R.B.	Clay Cross
II Steam tramway locomotives			
Wantage No. 5	1857	Wantage U.D.C.	Didcot, Berks.
Portstewart No. 1	1882	Hull Corporation	Hull Transport Museum
Portstewart No. 2	1883	Belfast Corporation	Belfast Transport Museum
Beyer Peacock No. 2	1885	Beyer Peacock & Co.	Crich Tramway Museum (on loan)

	Date Built	Owner	Location
*Manchester, Bury, Rochdale and Oldham No. 84	1886	Manchester College of Technology	Manchester

III Steam tramway trailers

*Dundee No. 2 (body only)	1888	A. W. Brotchie	Kellas, Angus

IV Electric tramcars

Giant's Causeway trailer No. 5	1883	Belfast Corporation	Belfast Transport Museum
Blackpool No. 1	1885	T.M.S.	Museum of British Transport, Clapham (on loan)
Bessbrook & Newry No. 2	1885	Belfast Corporation	Belfast Transport Museum
Douglas Southern No. 1	1896	B.R.B.	Museum of British Transport, Clapham
Glasgow No. 672	1898	Glasgow Corporation	Glasgow Transport Museum
Blackpool and Fleetwood No. 2	1898	T.M.S.	Crich Tramway Museum
Sheffield No. 46	1899	T.M.S.	Crich Tramway Museum
Glasgow No. 779	1900	Glasgow Corporation	Glasgow Transport Museum
Glasgow No. 812	1900	T.M.S.	Crich Tramway Museum
*Leeds No. 6 (ex Hull No. 96)	1900	A. J. Brown	Near Leeds
*Bolton No. 66	1901	66 Group	Belmont, Lancs.
*Dublin Directors' car	1901	H. K. Porter	Barnhill Road, Dalkey
Glasgow No. 585	1901	Science Museum, London	Science Museum, Exhibition Road, London, S.W.7
Hill of Howth No. 2	1901	Orange Empire Trolley Museum	Orange Empire Trolley Museum, Perris, California, U.S.A.
Hill of Howth No. 4	1901	Belfast Corporation	Belfast Transport Museum
*Hill of Howth No. 9	1902	Transport Museum Society of Ireland	Monkstown, Co. Dublin
Hill of Howth No. 10	1902	T.M.S.	Crich Tramway Museum
Newcastle No. 102	1901	T.M.S.	Byker, Newcastle
Blackpool No. 59	1902	T.M.S.	Crich Tramway Museum
Glasgow No. 488	1903	A.M.T.U.I.R.	Paris Transport Museum, 152 Boulevard Gabriel Péri, Malakoff (Seine)
*Derby No. 1	1903	Derby Tramway Group	Plumtree
*Nelson No. 4	1903	M. Harrison	Barrowford
Southampton No. 45	1903	T.M.S.	Crich Tramway Museum

	Date Built	Owner	Location
*London Transport No. 022	1903	T.M.S.	Woolwich
Glasgow No. 1017 (body only)	1904	I. L. Cormack	Cambuslang
Leicester No. 76	1904	T.M.S.	Crich Tramway Museum
Lowestoft No. 14	1904	East Anglia Transport Museum Society	East Anglia Transport Museum, Carlton Colville, Lowestoft
Belfast No. 249	1905	Belfast Corporation	Belfast Transport Museum
Cardiff No. 131	1905	T.M.S.	Crich Tramway Museum
Johannesburg No. 60	1905	T.M.S.	Crich Tramway Museum
Glasgow No. 21	1905	T.M.S.	Crich Tramway Museum
Prague No. 180	1905	T.M.S.	Crich Tramway Museum
Glasgow Mains Dept. No. 1	1906	T.M.S.	Crich Tramway Museum
*Sheffield No. 342	1907	North East Regional Museum	Consett, Co. Durham
London Transport No. 1025	1908	B.R.B.	Museum of British Transport, Clapham
London Transport No. 290	1910	B.R.B.	Museum of British Transport, Clapham
Hull No. 132	1910	T.M.S.	Crich Tramway Museum
Birmingham No. 395	1912	Birmingham Corporation	Museum of Science and Industry, Newhall Street, Birmingham, 3
*Manchester No. 765	1913	M.T.M.S. (body)/ T.M.S. (trucks)	Birchfields Road Depot, Manchester
Llandudno and Colwyn Bay No. 6	1914	B.R.B.	Museum of British Transport, Clapham
Blackpool and Fleetwood No. 40	1914	T.M.S.	Crich Tramway Museum
*Grimsby and Immingham No. 14	1915	T.M.S.	Clay Cross
Paisley No. 68	1919	T.M.S.	Crich Tramway Museum
Gateshead No. 52	1920	T.M.S.	Crich Tramway Museum
Sheffield No. 330	1920	T.M.S.	Crich Tramway Museum
Cheltenham No. 21	1921	T.M.S.	Crich Tramway Museum
Leeds No. 345	1921	T.M.S.	Crich Tramway Museum
Glasgow No. 22	1922	T.M.S.	Crich Tramway Museum
Glasgow No. 1088	1924	Glasgow Corporation	Glasgow Transport Museum
Blackpool No. 147	1924	Columbia Park and Southwestern	Near Cleveland, U.S.A.
Blackpool No. 144	1925	Seashore Electric Railway	Seashore Trolley Museum, Kennebunkport, Maine 04046, U.S.A.
*Gateshead No. 10	1925	North East Regional Museum	Consett, Co. Durham
*Bradford No. 104	1925	Bradford Corporation	Thornbury Works, Bradford

	Date Built	Owner	Location
Leeds No. 399	1925	T.M.S.	Crich Tramway Museum
Blackpool No. 40	1926	T.M.S.	Crich Tramway Museum
Blackpool No. 49	1926	T.M.S.	Crich Tramway Museum
Glasgow No. 1089	1926	Glasgow Corporation	Glasgow Transport Museum
Blackpool loco-motive	1927	T.M.S.	Crich Tramway Museum
Blackpool grinder No. 2	1927	T.M.S.	Crich Tramway Museum
Blackpool No. 158	1927	T.M.S.	Crich Tramway Museum
Blackpool No. 159	1927	East Anglia Transport Museum Society	Carlton Colville, Lowestoft
Gateshead No. 5	1927	T.M.S.	Crich Tramway Museum
Blackpool No. 48	1928	Oregon Electric Railway Historical Society	Glenwood, Oregon, U.S.A.
Glasgow No. 1100	1928	T.M.S.	Crich Tramway Museum
Glasgow No. 1115	1928	T.M.S.	Crich Tramway Museum
Blackpool No. 167	1928	T.M.S.	Crich Tramway Museum
*Swansea and Mumbles No. 2	1928	Middleton Railway Preservation Society	Park Side, Leeds
*Rotterdam No. 408	1929	J. L. Bowes	Near Maidstone
Belfast No. 357	1930	Belfast Corporation	Belfast Transport Museum
London Transport No. 1858	1930	P. J. Davis	East Anglia Transport Museum, Carlton Colville, Lowestoft, Suffolk
Sunderland No. 100 (M.E.T. No. 331)	1930	T.M.S.	Crich Tramway Museum
*Leeds No. 160	1931	Leeds Corporation	Park Side, Leeds
Leeds No. 180	1931	T.M.S.	Crich Tramway Museum
M.E.T. No. 355	1931	B,R.B.	Museum of British Transport, Clapham
London Transport No. 2085	1931	Seashore Electric Railway	Seashore Trolley Museum, U.S.A.
*Leeds tower car	1932	Leeds Tramway Historical Society	Garforth, Yorks.
Leeds No. 301 (L.C.C. No. 1)	1932	B.R.B.	Museum of British Transport, Clapham
Sheffield No. 189	1934	T.M.S.	Crich Tramway Museum
*Liverpool No. 869	1936	T.M.S.	Green Lane, Liverpool
Sheffield No. 264	1937	T.M.S.	Crich Tramway Museum
Glasgow No. 1173	1938	Glasgow Corporation	Glasgow Transport Museum
*Liverpool No. 245	1938	Liverpool Corporation	Edge Lane Works, Liverpool
*Blackpool No. 11	1939	East Anglia Transport Museum Society	Carlton Colville, Lowestoft
Liverpool No. 293	1939	Seashore Electric Railway	Seashore Trolley Museum, U.S.A.

	Date Built	Owner	Location
Glasgow No. 1245	1939	A. H. Gordon	Carlton Colville, Lowestoft
Glasgow No. 1274	1940	Seashore Electric Railway	Seashore Trolley Museum, U.S.A.
Glasgow No. 1282	1940	T.M.S.	Crich Tramway Museum
Edinburgh No. 35	1948	Edinburgh Corporation	Edinburgh Municipal Transport Museum
Glasgow No. 1297	1948	T.M.S.	Crich Tramway Museum
Sheffield No. 510	1950	T.M.S.	Crich Tramway Museum
*Sheffield No. 513	1950	T.M.S.	Crich Tramway Museum
Glasgow No. 1392	1952	B.R.B.	Museum of British Transport, Clapham
Leeds No. 602	1953	T.M.S.	Crich Tramway Museum
Leeds No. 600	1954	T.M.S.	Crich Tramway Museum

BIBLIOGRAPHY

Periodicals include:

Modern Tramway (Ian Allan and Light Railway Transport League)
Tramway Review (Light Railway Transport League)
Omnibus Magazine (Omnibus Society)
Tramway Museum Society Journal
Transport World
Passenger Transport
Modern Transport

General books include:

The Golden Age of Tramways, Charles Klapper (Routledge and Kegan Paul 1961)
Great British Tramway Networks, W. H. Bett and J. C. Gillham (Light Railway Transport League 1962)
The British Tram, Frank E. Wilson (Percival Marshall 1961)
Veteran and Vintage Tramcars, J. H. Price (Ian Allan 1963)
Tramway Twilight, J. Joyce (Ian Allan 1962)

Publications on specific undertakings include:

The Tramways of Accrington, R. W. Rush (Light Railway Transport League 1961). Includes also Blackburn and Darwen
ABC of Birmingham City Transport Trams and Trolleybuses, W. A. Camwell (Ian Allan 1950)
By Tram to the Tower: 80 Years of Blackpool Tramways, G. S. Palmer (author 1965)
North Station and Fleetwood, G. S. Palmer (Blackpool and Fylde Tramway Historical Association 1963)
The Tramways of Bournemouth and Poole, R. C. Anderson (Light Railway Transport League 1964)
Cheltenham's Trams and Buses, J. B. Appleby and F. Lloyd (21 Tram Group 1964)
Edinburgh's Transport, D. L. G. Hunter (Advertiser Press 1964)
The Tramways of Gateshead, George S. Hearse (author 1965)
Glasgow's Trams (Glasgow Museum of Transport 1964)
A Handbook of Glasgow Tramways, D. L. Thomson (Scottish Tramway Museum Society 1962)
The Last Tram, Charles A. Oakley (Glasgow Corporation 1962)
Green Goddesses Go East, Ian L. Cormack (Scottish Tramway Museum Society 1961)
The Tramways of Huddersfield, Roy Brook (Advertiser Press 1959)
Isle of Man Album, W. J. Wyse and J. Joyce (Ian Allan 1968)

The Narrow Gauge Railways of Ireland, H. Fayle (Greenlake Publications 1946)

Leeds City Tramways: A Pictorial Souvenir, Robert F. Mack (Turntable Enterprises 1968)

Public Transport in Leicester (Leicester Museum and Leicester City Transport 1961)

Leicester's Trams, K. W. Smith (Light Railway Transport League 1964)

Liverpool Tramways 1943–1957, R. E. Blackburn (Light Railway Transport League 1968)

The ABC of London Transport Trams and Trolleybuses, S. L. Poole (Ian Allan 1948)

The London Tramcar 1861–1951, R. W. Kidner (Oakwood Press 1951)

London Bus and Tram Album, V. H. Darling (Ian Allan 1967)

The Tramways of Croydon, 'Southmet' (Light Railway Transport League 1960)

The Tramways of East London, 'Rodinglea' (Light Railway Transport League 1967)

The Felthams, K. C. Blacker (Dryhurst Publications 1962)

The Manchester Tram, Ian Yearsley (Advertiser Press 1962)

Manchester Corporation Transport Department Diamond Jubilee (Manchester Corporation 1961)

The Tramways of Northumberland, George S. Hearse (author 1961)

Tramways of the West of England, P. W. Gentry (Light Railway Transport League 1960)

The Tramways of Portsmouth, S. E. Harrison (Light Railway Transport League 1963)

The Tramways of Salford, E. Gray (Manchester Transport Historical Collection 1963)

British Tramways in Pictures: 1. Sheffield, R. J. S. Wiseman (Advertiser Press 1964)

The Tramways of Sunderland, S. A. Staddon (Advertiser Press 1964)

The First Passenger Railway: The Swansea and Mumbles Railway, Charles E. Lee (Railway Publishing Company 1942)

Volk's Railway, Alan A. Jackson (Light Railway Transport League 1963)

INDEX